HELP, GOD!

I CAN'T AFFORD A PSYCHIATRIST!

HELP, GOD!

I CAN'T AFFORD A PSYCHIATRIST!

How I (finally!) stopped looking for my Daddy hero In all the wrong places (including church)

DONNA BENEDICT

 Suncoast Digital Press, Inc.

ISBN 978-1-964143-04-0

▊▊ Suncoast Digital Press, Inc.
Sarasota, Florida

Printed in the United States of America

Unless otherwise noted, Scripture quotations are taken from
the Holy Bible, *New International Version, NIV.*

CONTENTS

Born in Brooklyn, I'm Daddy's girl!

DEDICATION

To my father, Donald Thibodeau,
who taught me true love and compassion,
which led me to the eternal love
of my Heavenly Father

PREFACE

Over 20 years ago, I was impressed upon to write my story through the Holy Spirit. It was a sudden realization which had me understand this was important, of value, and deserved my consideration. In May of 2024 during my prayer time, I heard the Holy Spirit whisper, "It's time...write your book."

If you have the slightest inkling that my account of hearing that direct encouragement from God is true, then this book is for you. I'm not here to preach, explain why you're going to hell, or promote one Christian church over another. Others may be called to do that, but my goal is simple: Let my story fill you with hope and optimism that you can restore or build a vital connection with God.

This book is written in two parts, "Life Before Christ is Really Hard" and "Life After Christ is Really Hard." This should assure you that I'm not proposing that being a follower of Christ will magically smooth out every wrinkle in your life, prevent hardships, or grant your deepest wishes. Life happens—yet, I can tell you first-hand that having Jesus by your side is a tremendous help through it all. Many people I've talked with want to believe that—and perhaps did believe that at one time. And then something happened that shattered their trust. I'll share my versions of that in the following chapters. Yes, at different times, my faith was shattered, battered, and tattered.

I will speak to you, the dear woman or man who walks into church with devastating hurts, trauma, sickness, fear, shame, or guilt from past and present traumatic experiences. Many of us are met with, "Don't speak negatively, you'll speak your pain into existence." For others, as soon as they share their deepest sin and ask for help, they find their confidence has been broken. The "safe" person, whether a counselor, "friend," or pastor, has spread gossip throughout the church. Some of us have even been sexually violated by a church leader. Feelings of betrayal and mistrust push you out of church and sometimes even further into sin. In some cases, even away from God. Believe me, I've been there and it is devastating when you're desperately looking for help.

These stories are my real-life situations, the good, bad and the ugly. Trying to find help from the church was futile. From suicidal ideations to nearly dying of an overdose, I searched for a way out of my pain—and someone, anyone…to love me unconditionally. I finally found Him. Like the prodigal son/daughter, He drew me into His open arms for me to surrender to His unconditional love and forgiveness. Dirty, broken, full of sorrow and open wounds seemingly too deep to heal, my Heavenly Father, through Jesus Christ and the Holy Spirit, began the healing process in my heart.

I was recently told that I had a lot of courage to write this memoir with nothing held back, but I immediately thought about you, the person who has the courage to open their heart and mind, to seek truth, to take a step towards God instead of away from Him. You're my inspiration. Through my story, I believe you will see that your Heavenly Father is loving, forgiving, and compassionate. He desires to walk with you in the midst of painful circumstances. Psalms 34:19: "Many are the afflictions of the righteous: But the LORD delivers him out of them all." This is a promise we can all stand on.

Help, God!

Part I

Life Before Christ...
Is Really Hard

Help, God!

1

A Child's First Lessons

I wake up and it's dark and quiet. When I hear a faint sound from down the hall, I know why my sleep was interrupted.

Dad doesn't sleep very well. I get up from bed and quietly tip-toe down the hall, careful to avoid the creaking places on the floor—I certainly don't want to wake up my mother. In the quiet of the still, late hour, he is absorbed in thought. He's the Display Manager at David's Women's Clothing store where he decorates the windows and the inside of the store for the seasons and holidays.

He looks up and greets me with the kindest smile. "HI honey, what are you doing up?" he asks.

"It's hot in my bedroom and I couldn't sleep," I respond.

He pulls a chair over next to him and I sit in my favorite spot – up close to my dad. Sitting here, I watch him drawing his designs on top of the smooth surface of our Formica-top table. With pencil in hand, he makes quick lines—drawing, erasing, drawing, erasing.

He is sketching out his design ideas for the next creative thing he wants to use in one of his window displays. I watch quietly, fascinated as he brings his ideas to life. He is an incredible artist, and I absolutely love his designs and creativity. I can't wait to actually see them in the store window. He dresses the manikins in the latest fashions and they almost look real, coming alive in vivid colors and textures. Surrounded with the designs he's created from the designs drawn on the kitchen table, he builds the set to fit the season. It's like magic.

It's so special spending a few quiet moments with him and I cherish every second. No noise and commotion, just a few minutes of peace and quiet. Being the oldest of eight kids, I still know I'm "Daddy's little girl." He is and always will be my hero. He's my compassionate, loving protector in my otherwise intolerable life.

My first vivid memory of Dad is when I'm about four or five years old. We had just moved to Albany. He comes home from work early, sits on the floor, puts me on his lap, and I see tears in his eyes. He apologizes for punishing me for something I did wrong.

"Donna, I'm so sorry for having to spank you this morning. It hurt me more than it hurt you, I think. What you did was wrong and to protect you from ever doing it again, I had to spank you. I don't ever want to see you get hurt because you disobeyed what I told you to do."

I don't remember the spanking or what the punishment was for. His love, compassion and tears for me while holding me on his lap and hugging me close to his chest, crowd out all memory of the spanking. After this, I know I never want to hurt him ever again. He's my daddy and I love him more than anything. He

4

consistently shows me how much he loves and cares for me and I am so thankful for my wonderful, loving dad.

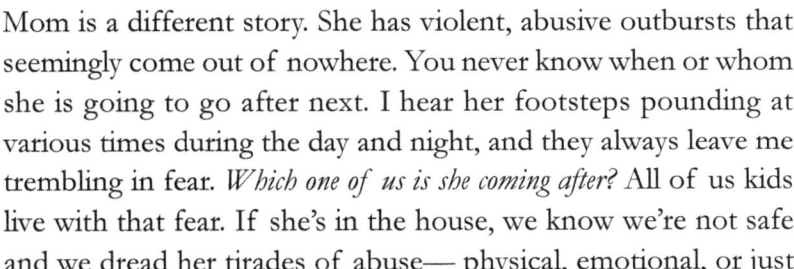

Mom is a different story. She has violent, abusive outbursts that seemingly come out of nowhere. You never know when or whom she is going to go after next. I hear her footsteps pounding at various times during the day and night, and they always leave me trembling in fear. *Which one of us is she coming after?* All of us kids live with that fear. If she's in the house, we know we're not safe and we dread her tirades of abuse— physical, emotional, or just ear-piercing fury. She has severe emotional problems, but as a little girl, all I know is that she scares me to death.

Dad left for work. I'm in my room that Pat and I share. *Oh God, no.* I hear her coming. Uh oh, my heart starts racing. I feel the terror rising up within me and I'm totally unaware of what Pat is going through. She barges in, rips the clothes out of our closet, throwing them in a heap on the floor. Then she dumps out our dresser drawers, flinging clothes all around the room. I watch in horror, hoping beyond hope that she'll sweep the last item, my jewelry box, off the dresser and leave. But she doesn't leave. She starts screaming, reaches for Pat, grabs her by the hair, and hits her in the face, over and over and over. She turns to me, grabs my hair and starts shaking me back and forth like a rag doll, "Donna, you're a pig! Look at what a mess this room is!"

"Clean up this mess and get yourselves ready for school. I want this room clean before you leave this house," she commands. We fly into action, picking up clothes and reorganizing our room as fast as we can so we can get dressed and out the door for school.

I feel disconnected from my body. My mind is numb and even after I get to class, I can't focus or concentrate.

When I'm away from her, at school, or in a restaurant, I catch myself tensing up my shoulders, and constantly looking behind and around me for fear of being attacked by someone, anyone. I'm so used to bracing for an attack that I can't let my guard down; I can never relax. All of my siblings are affected as well. We never know when she will fly into a rage, keeping us on guard constantly.

Mysteriously, there's another side of Mom that is over-the-top generous and fun. This leaves us in a tortuous place of uncertainty, hoping for the good side to emerge, while fearing the appearance of her cruel Mrs. Hyde.

Thanksgiving, Christmas and other celebratory events bring out her sane and caring side. She makes sure Christmas is special for all of us. Each one of us have at least ten or more gifts under the tree. Decorating, wrapping presents for one and all. Mom and Dad have big families, so there's at least 50 or more people that gather together to exchange gifts. Birthday parties, wedding showers, or baby showers, she's in the middle of them all. She makes cakes with her delicious homemade frostings. Her famous Hershey's fudge is sheer perfection, and we can't wait to consume the S'mores she makes over the gas stove. She attends every outing, birthday party, wedding, funeral, and such. At these, she is amiable and usually the "life of the party." Several of my cousins love her as their favorite aunt, completely sold on her act of being the perfect mom. They have no idea.

In addition to her acting and social entertaining skills, she actually does a good job managing the household budget. She only has a seventh-grade education, but I can't believe how she can stretch a penny. We always have nice clothes, dinner on the table every night and a warm bed to sleep in, no matter what. She starts Christmas shopping in June, puts everything on layaway, and has it all paid off before Christmas. I appreciate how she takes care of her family this way.

What I really want most from Mom is her love when it isn't Christmas or my birthday. I can't help but compare her to my dad and how he makes me feel safe, cared for, and respected. Beginning at a young age, my relationship with her is strained and dysfunctional. I don't trust her; I love and hate her at the same time. Her love is what I want most of all, but I'm not sure I will ever have it. There's a part of me that thinks she loves me but I'm never quite sure. Practically right out of the crib I hear her say to me, "You will never amount to anything. You can't do anything right. You're stupid." I begin to believe that everything she says about me is true and I will never measure up to her standards.

Hurt, anger, bitterness, and resentment become deep-rooted within me, caused by the cruel words she carelessly flings about when she's mad about who knows what. How can I go on living this way? Terrified, I believe that if someone finds out how we live they will know it's all my fault. All I want is a way to escape the insanity I feel because of her. I want to run away, but I'm young and don't know where to go. Besides, I love my dad, and he's the one who keeps me protected. Problem is, he isn't always here. He doesn't know the half of what we endure. I only wish someone did.

"Cruel words erode the self-esteem like the ocean eats away the shore."

—Abigail Van Buren

It's a beautiful, Saturday morning, I'm 10 years old and feeling quite grown up because I spent the night at a friend's house. I had a great time with her lovely family, and now I'm heading back home. I'm carrying my little suitcase and skipping along towards the city bus stop, filled with happiness and peace. If my bus isn't there, my friend instructed me to go into the little grocery store at the bus stop to wait. Not seeing my bus, I climb up the step leading to the front door of the store, push it open and walk inside. The walls are a pea green color with accents of yellow here and there. The floor is tiled with a variegated yellow and green pattern. *Ugly!* is all that comes to mind.

There's a counter to my left with a glass enclosure that displays different candies, gum, and a variety of treats. The cash register sits on top of the counter. To my right are several tall shelves filled with canned goods, cereals, and a variety of other items.

A short, stocky old man is standing next to the counter. I know who he is. No one else is here; we are alone. I put down my suitcase. The old man is walking towards me and as soon as my hand releases the handle, he grabs my arm! He jerks me over and pulls me between two of the shelves.

We are hidden from the front door. I am shocked and my whole body freezes. I'm terrified like a deer in the headlights. I can't move. He wraps his arms around my body so I'm facing him. He smells like an old cigar and dried sour sweat. He grabs my butt with both hands and pulls me tightly so I'm pressed up against him. My feet come up off the floor. I'm frozen in fear and can't react. He tries to stick his tongue in my mouth and just then the shopkeeper's bell over the inside of the front door jingles loudly and someone walks in.

Immediately he drops me, and as fast as I can, I dash out from between the shelves, grab my suitcase and bolt out the door. *Thank God there's a bus! I don't care if this is my bus, I'm getting on.* It's just idling there with no driver, but I don't care. The two front steps are pretty steep but I jump with all my might, landing on the top step. *I forgot to put in my token. I don't care.* I get on my hands and knees and begin to crawl towards the back of the bus. The black rubber mat on the floor is covered in dirt and grit. My pretty dress doesn't keep the grit from digging into my legs and knees with every move. *Ouch, don't cry. Keep going.*

Finally, I reach the last dark green seat on the side of the bus that faces the store. As I crawl under the seat, I pull my suitcase in with me and press it close against my trembling body so we are totally hidden.

My heart is pounding out of my chest, and I feel like I want to throw up. Several minutes seems like several hours. The bus isn't moving. *Where is that bus driver? God, please be with me. I'm so afraid of what that old man will do if he finds me.* Slowly I rise up just enough to peek out the window. That evil old man is standing in front of the store. His hands are on his hips and he's looking up and down the street. I'm sure he's looking for me. *Where's that guy who walked into the store just in the nick of time? I don't see him anywhere. That's odd.* Ducking back under the seat, I wait. The bus driver, finally! I hear a loud "whoosh" noise as the door closes and the bus starts to move away from the curb. *God, please don't let that old man follow me home.*

Crawling out from under the seat, I climb up onto it and sit down, keeping my head low, but keeping an eye out for my stop. Thank God, here's where I get off. The door at the back of the bus opens with another "whoosh" and I grab my suitcase, run to the steps, and leap off the bus. I land with a thud on the sidewalk. My mind is in a swirl of fear on so many levels and I can't think straight. *I can't tell my mother. She will kill him. She*

> I can't tell my mother. She will kill him. She won't let me stay overnight with my friend ever again.

won't let me stay overnight with my friend ever again. There's no way I can tell Dad either, because he'll tell Mom and I know she'll punish me. Terror hits me at the thought of walking in the house to face her. My fear of her is almost greater than my fear of that old man. I just know, even at ten years old, that it will not go well if I tell her or anybody.

Walking up the steps to the front of my house, I hesitate, take a deep breath and open the door. The small vestibule is dark when I enter. I turn the corner to walk into the living room. My mother is sitting on the couch with one leg tucked under the other as she looks out the sun-filled bay windows that oversee the front porch. She looks at me and motions for me to sit with her. Reluctantly, I walk over and sit down. I can tell by the frown on her face she is upset about something. She says, "Donna, what's wrong, you're white as a sheet?"

"Nothing, I'm okay," I say, even though my stomach is tied in knots. *She knows something is wrong, but I will never tell.* I keep my mouth tightly shut. She continues to question me. I can't think, feel, or respond. Staring at her, all I want to do is get up, go in the bathroom, throw up, then go to my room.

11

Finally, she realizes her questions will get no answers. She tells me to get up and put my things away. Like a robot, I get up off the couch, walk through the living room, the dining room, and turn to go into my bedroom. Closing the door behind me, I drop my suitcase on the floor and throw myself down on my bed. I bury my head into my pillow and sob quietly, trembling from head to toe. *I will never go near that dirty old man ever again. I hate him. I hate what he did to me.*

Gone is any sense of safety and peace. I'm not safe around anyone, anywhere. I'm 10 and now I know: The world is not safe. I will never tell anyone what happened. I think, *I don't like how he made me feel. Would he have hurt me more if the other person hadn't come in the front door?* My whole body is still trembling. *Was this my fault? Did I ask for him do this to me somehow?*

I recover enough to fake it through dinner with my family. It takes everything I have to act "normal" as my body begins to settle down. After dinner, Pat and I go outside and sit on the front porch. We decide to grab our bikes and ride around the block. Thankful to escape the glaring eyes of my mother, it feels good to get out and feel the fresh, crisp air blow against my face as we ride and ride around that block until we're both worn out.

Here it is, a year after that old man stole my innocence. At the time, I could not have known that it wouldn't be the last time I was molested. Our family dentist and a female babysitter stole another part of my childhood innocence. The same "deer in the headlights" reaction hit me. The fear paralyzes me.

The effects of these molestations haunt me. The old man is a friend of the family. The babysitter is a relative and I'm around her frequently. How can I get free of the "fear and terror" I feel when I see them or anyone who reminds me of them? Will I ever get over the shock, terror, shame, and guilt? I hold all of this deep inside. It's in the shadow of my inner chamber of secrets. Nobody knows, and I don't think I can or will tell anyone.

Reliving the memories, all I can do is live one day at a time the best I can, cautiously looking over my shoulder. Whenever anyone like that old man gets close, I leave the room, the sidewalk or store, all the while looking behind to be sure I am not being followed. *Help, God! Keep these awful people away from me. Help me stay safe, even from my mother.*

Help, God!

2

Winter Ups and Downs

It's 1961. The city of Albany, New York, is the greatest place in the world as far as I'm concerned. Parties with our friends, dances at both the Catholic school and Christian Boys Academy always give me something to look forward to. Buses, cabs, Woolworths, candy stores filled with yummy treats, museums, and the State Capitol. Even at 12 years old I'm growing up to love being a city girl.

We have lots of snow in the winter. Ice skating, sledding, and peaceful walks in the cold, brisk snow help me through the frigid winter months. When the snowflakes hit the streetlights in the evening, it's like crystals glowing against the night sky. Summers are hot, muggy, and buggy. Bugs are my least favorite of all creatures on this earth. Spiders, grasshoppers, June bugs, BEES – why did God create these horrible things? Pat, Debby, and I spend a lot of time outside roller skating, playing hide-and-seek, jump rope, or riding our bikes. Pat and I love to take long walks around the city (in any season) to escape our chaotic and abusive home life.

Moving Right Along

Mom and Dad decide to move us out of the public school system to attend the Catholic school. It's the beginning of 7th grade and the transition is very difficult. Geography, Algebra, and diagramming sentences are subjects I did not study in public school. *I'm really stupid. I'm failing at everything. I will never amount to anything.* These beliefs run through my mind constantly. Luckily, I do have one part of the day I love—my favorite class is religion. Learning about God and what it means to be Catholic consumes my thoughts. I love reading books about the saints and how they suffered for Christ. I'm starting to love the Virgin Mary, who seems so pure, kind, and religious.

Even though I'm an extremely shy kid, I become very fast friends with Barbara and Grace who are in my class. We are outcasts because we don't hang with the "in crowd." The three of us are shy and somewhat immature for our age. Dressed in a navy blue uniform with a white blouse underneath a jumper, I don't have to worry about what to wear to school. Makeup is not allowed, our hair isn't teased up to the ceiling, and we still love to play with Barbie dolls and toys for little girls.

Barbara, Grace, my sister Patty and I walk together around the city. We love to walk to Central Avenue where all the boys hang out. We excitedly pop into Woolworth's to sit at the counter and order a Coke. I love to watch the clink of those little square ice cubes as they hit the side of the glass.

We hang around the makeup counters, acting too giddy for our age. With our babysitting money, we buy eye shadow, lipstick, eyeliner, and mascara that Grace takes home to hide in her closet until our next trip out.

We head for the Woolworth bathroom, stand in front of the mirror, and encourage one another to put on make-up as heavy as we dare. I draw on thick black eyeliner, tease up my hair with a rat-tail comb, spray it with Aqua-Net, and watch as the other girls put on their eye shadow and lipstick. Now we are ready to head out, all made-up and prancing around Central Avenue to flirt with the good-looking guys who walk around looking for girls to flirt with. The boys are always polite, friendly, and very protective of us. We feel perfectly safe in their company even though we don't know them very well.

Before our walk home, back into the Woolworth bathroom we go. We comb out our hair and wash off the makeup. Just kids enjoying the freedom of living in the big city. These girls and our fun times together bring me a sense of peace and joy, sans violence, screaming, and humiliation. Taking a deep breath, I walk into my house. *Please God, keep my mother from beating me up tonight.* I sure hope my prayer gets answered.

They Call it Puppy Love

A beautiful purebred beagle, Fritzi comes along with us almost everywhere we go, and we love him like he's a family member. He's allowed to roam free. He doesn't chase cars and doesn't bark unless he senses danger. He follows us to school, to church, and takes walks with us. He's made friends with our school's nuns and priests and is allowed to come into my classroom, where he sits or lies by my desk until it's time for us to walk home. Even the nuns love Fritzi. He is a constant companion for us, like a little brother. When he's around, I feel safer and more relaxed than usual—maybe it's his unconditional love, his predictably good nature, his desire to simply be my companion. He has no idea how much I count on him.

Today is Sunday and I'm all dressed up in a light blue sheath dress, my first pair of high heels, white gloves, and I'm wearing my mantilla to cover my head. At mass, I'm seated in the back row when, all of a sudden, I see Fritzi racing up the center aisle of the church! He romps across the middle of the altar towards Father Cox, wagging his tail in excitement to see this priest he knows so well. Father Cox is standing behind the altar and has the Communion bread raised up towards the ceiling. (This is very significant to Catholics because it means the priest believes he is now transforming the bread into the literal body and blood of Jesus.) Father Cox doesn't acknowledge Fritzi in the midst of this solemn moment, so the little pup starts jumping up and down and pawing at his leg for attention. I cannot believe what I'm seeing.

Then, an usher crouches low and scurries across the altar to grab Fritzi's collar and lead him out a nearby side door. Mortified, I quickly get up and rush out the back door. I walk home as quickly as possible like nothing happened. Fritzi is already home when I get there. That evening, Father Cox arrives at the house to join us for dinner. I'm not sure what the conversation entails, but I don't remember Fritzi ever following me to church again after that day. How I chuckle to myself every time I think about Fritzi jumping up and down at Father Cox in the middle of mass.

It's a blizzard and schools are closed. My siblings and I are thrilled to get to stay home because of all the snow and ice.

We six girls and our parents crowd into occupying the downstairs of a two-story house. The largest room has beautiful wooden columns separating the living room area from the dining room. My bedroom is off of the dining room. Walking out of my room, I turn the corner and head towards the kitchen. Out of nowhere, I feel a violent blow to the back of my head, followed by pain, but mostly dizziness. I realize that my mother, with her full force, hit me on the side of the head. It felt like a punch even though it was her open hand.

The room spins and I try to keep myself from falling to the floor. She moves in front of me, points her finger in my face, and says, "That's because I love you." Stunned, I push the tears down into the recesses of my belly. The pain and swelling begin at the back of my head and my neck is throbbing. *What did I do to deserve this? I didn't even hear her come up behind me.* I am confused, thinking maybe I did do something wrong, but I don't dare say a word.

"You look like a little hussy," she says, spitting out her words. "Look at the way you're dressed. You're so stupid, you'll never amount to anything." Angry, hate-filled words spew out of her mouth. Her nose is wrinkled, brows furrowed and her face is contorted into the meanest scowl I've ever seen. She looks like a witch. I can almost hear her saying, "*I'll get you my little pretty, and your little dog, Fritzi, too!*"

Filled with shame, I think, *What did I do? Why is she raging at me? I must have done something she hates...*

I'm also mad at myself for not hearing her come up behind me— I've gotten good at cringing away, ducking, and bracing. I try my best not to think about the devastating things that happen to me, abuse both outside and inside my home. It makes me feel sad

19

and like maybe I really am the loser my mother keeps telling me I am. I'm pretty hard on myself, that's for sure. *I'm stupid. I can't do anything right. I must have caused the abuse somehow. Did I flirt with those who molested me because I'm a hussy? Did I dress wrong or move my body wrong somehow?* The abuse piles up, one incident after another... one incident goes on top of the last one and pushes the other ones down into a deep abyss within me. I'm so full and so empty at the same time.

I obsess about how to escape. Forgetfulness and denial creep in. Sexual fantasies and masturbation are fleeting comforts. Maybe I'll join the convent. Or I could run away to California, but I love Albany—I just hate the nightmarish part of my life.

Daddy's home. I wake up abruptly from my nap on the couch. My daddy, my hero and protector is walking in the door from work. My siblings and I jump up and down yelling, "Daddy's home, Daddy's home!" With glee I watch as he approaches Mom, smiling as he wraps his arms around her, hugs her, and kisses her on the cheek. A few minutes go by, then he comes over to me, wraps his arms around me and rubs his five o'clock shadow into my neck. It tickles and I give him a hug to welcome him home. After he hugs each one of us, he walks over to the coffee table that sits in front of the sofa in our living room. We all pile around the table and watch as he places a box of Fanny Farmer candy on the table. We all squeal at the sight of our favorite toffee candy. It's smothered in chocolate and peanuts. Pieces of the crunchy peanuts lie in the bottom of the box, but are quickly snatched up by several pairs of hands. What a special treat he brings home for all of us to share.

There is no doubt in my mind that my daddy loves me. I know he loves all of his girls, but I really crave his love, compassion and the care he gives me as his daughter. It's hard to describe how much mutual respect I can tell we have for each other. *How can I be so lucky to have him as my dad?* For that, I am very happy.

———————◇———————

It's November 22, 1963. I am 14 years old and a freshman in high school and I have five younger sisters and Mom is pregnant for number seven. On my walk home from school, with my transistor radio playing my favorite music, news interrupts the song "He's So Fine" by the Chiffons. "President Kennedy has been shot…"*Oh My GOD*. I race as fast as I can down the block to get home. Running up the stairs of our front porch, I grab the front door, fling it open and slam it behind me as I bound into the house. I yell through the living room, "Mom quick turn on the TV. President Kennedy has been shot." She comes into the living room with a frown on her face. Her lips are pursed together and I can just tell by her look that she doesn't believe me. Rushing over to the TV, I turn it on as the news is broadcast across the black and white screen. Walter Cronkite sits at his news desk with a somber expression and delivers the devastating news.

PRESIDENT KENNEDY IS DEAD. A hush settles over the house. Daddy walks in from work early and we are stunned by the horror as we watch the reruns of the events of the day. Our household is very quiet for several days.

On November 25, 1963, my mother's birthday, the family congregates in the living room. The Venetian blinds are closed, curtains are pulled, and all the lights are turned off. Mom and Dad are snuggled together on the couch. I'm sitting on the floor with my younger sisters scattered around the room. On the small black and white TV, we watch the funeral of a President we all love. My heart is broken for Jackie, his wife, little John, Jr., and Caroline. Such a senseless tragedy. A heavy grief creeps into my heart. *How does Jackie cope with the death of her husband? How tragic for John Jr. and Caroline. I hope I never have to deal with my daddy dying and leaving me and our family.* Every so often thoughts of losing my daddy at an early age creep into my mind. It terrifies me.

Life begins to settle down. One day at a time, one horrific abuse at a time, I try my best to cope. Nightmares haunt me. Terror strikes out of nowhere sometimes when I think of losing my dad. For now, I do my best to live my young life in Albany with my Catholic faith, family, friends and Fritzi.

Another late night and I suddenly wake up. Since I think I hear the TV, I get up to go join my dad. I'm 15 and still as close to Daddy as ever. I see my dad sitting on the couch watching Godzilla attacking a train. Even in black-and-white, it's pretty dramatic. The only light in the room is coming from the TV. As I come alongside the couch, my dad gives me a slight smile and gets up to turn the knob on the television, lowering the volume. I wonder why he did that as I sit down on the other end of the couch.

22

"Donna," he begins, "You probably didn't see it on the news, but a girl over in Altamont was attacked."

I know he doesn't mean by Godzilla, but the monster's image does come to mind.

"Dad! What happened?"

He hesitates a moment and then explains to me that she was raped. After confirming that I have a basic understanding of that violation, he says that I've got to be careful. I should not be anywhere by myself that doesn't feel safe, and furthermore, I should be aware that it can happen even by some boy I think I know. He doesn't go into anything more about my avoiding danger, just what to do if I find myself in that kind of big trouble. *I never told him about the evil, dirty old man. What does he know?*

I can't help but notice he is quite uncomfortable. This can't be an easy topic for him to bring up with his daughter. He's always been completely appropriate with my sisters and me, not even walking around the house in his underwear, and only giving warm fatherly hugs. Any discussion to do with sex, and now, the abuse of sex, embarrasses him—but his protective caring side is stronger than his discomfort, and so he continues.

He says he wants to tell me how to move and fight to protect myself if I get into the same situation as that poor girl. Dad says I must push the attacker away as hard as I can while writhing and keeping my pelvis rotating, my hips going back and forth, as I fight for all I'm worth.

I get the picture, but apparently, he wants to make it even more crystal clear. He gets off the sofa and walks over to the record player. His face is so red it looks like it's glowing in the dark. I stifle

23

a laugh as I watch him take a record out of its sleeve and place it on the turntable, switching it on so it starts spinning. With a pencil in hand, he tries to put the pencil into the middle of the moving hole. He turns and says, "It's like trying to put a pencil into the middle of the record while it's spinning. When you keep rotating your hips, you are working hard to keep yourself safe."

"Thank you, Daddy, I know this was hard for you," I say, hoping his angst will go away now that he's completed his demonstration and I have managed to not laugh out loud.

"I think this is something your mother should discuss with you, but she probably won't, and I feel it is my responsibility."

"Thank you, Dad, really. I love you and thank you for wanting to protect me. I'm really tired and I have to be up early for school so I'm going back to bed." I give him a hug and head back to my bedroom. As I'm dozing off, I feel so grateful for him, for his caring, and think how much I cherish spending time with him, even if it's snatched from the middle of the night with Godzilla in the background.

3

Moving Forward

The phone rings at 7 a.m. September 14, 1965. We are already up, quite anxious to hear news of our new sibling's arrival. With much excitement, I pick up the phone. Dad says, "It's a boy! And there ain't even a bar open!" After seven daughters, Dad finally welcomes a son.

When Mom and Gregg come home, you'd think it was a celebration of the Yankees winning the World Series. We're all happy to welcome our baby boy, but no one is more pleased than Dad. It's been three weeks and everyone is still in a good mood, even Mom.

I'm in the kitchen and she comes in after putting baby Gregg down for a nap. "Donna, we sold the house and we are moving out of Albany to a little suburb called Latham."

"What?!" Jumping up from my seat at the kitchen table, I start pacing back and forth, fighting to catch my breath.

I am very attached to everything about where we live, especially my friends and the Catholic school. "Mom, no!" My mind is racing, trying to come up with an alternative to this terrible fate. *How can I stay in Albany? Who can I live with? Do I have to move with you?*

There's no changing this plan, it's already in motion. It seems like I've only known for a few hours when the moving van pulls up in our driveway. Just seeing it makes it real and I feel like I just got punched in the stomach. The packers come in and get to work disassembling my life. The loaders remove everything so matter-of-factly, oblivious to how they are ripping up my life roots.

I can't stop it. Everything I've ever known is in this city. I'm terrified of the thought of going to a new school and a whole new lifestyle. It's the same state, yes, but it may as well be in Siberia. I'll be living in exile because even though Latham is only 30 minutes away from here, when you don't drive or have convenient public transportation, it might as well be across the ocean. I NEED to have a sense of belonging. I hate this news.

It's right before Christmas and we're here. The house is much bigger than the two-family one we moved from. There are three bedrooms and a bath upstairs. The main floor has the living room, dining room, kitchen, two bedrooms, and a full bath. Having five bedrooms is amazing, plus it has a full basement.

Our street is somewhat heavily traveled for a small suburb. In Albany, houses lined both sides of the narrow street and everyone parked along the street. Here in Latham, there's an empty field across the street and everyone parks their cars in the driveways in front of their house. Pat and I shared a small room in Albany, and we still share a room, though this one is much larger. I miss that little cozy room. I miss everything I've been uprooted from: the city sounds, sights and smells, and most of all, my best friends and our Catholic school. I feel like I've lost so much and am grieving over it all.

It's freezing cold as I stand in front of my house waiting for the school bus. I've never seen a school bus, much less been on one. It makes its way around the corner and I see this big, bright yellow bus slowing down, headed for our little group. It stops and my sister, a few neighborhood kids, and I climb the steps up into the bus. I was not expecting it to already be so full of kids. Loud kids, every one of them a stranger to me. Looking around to find a seat, my heart starts racing and nausea creeps into my stomach. *How many kids are on this thing? I want to get out.* I feel like I'm in a coffin, smothering. The smell of wet leather, wet snow, kids yelling and bouncing around the bus overloads my senses. I want to run off the bus, go back to bed, pull the covers over my head, and never come out. This has to be a dream. *Help, God, let this be a dream.*

My high school is comprised of the "middle-class kids," that's me, and the "wealthy-class kids." The middle-class kids are ridiculed and looked upon as "less than" because they are not rich. This doesn't feel right. I don't fit in. It's the middle of my junior year, I have no friends, and this is not my life. *I hate it here.*

Memories of my friends, city life, and the Catholic school begin to fade. I close off my love and longing for them so I don't lose my mind. I'm getting good at numbing pain…I've had plenty of practice. Unfortunately, when my head hits the pillow at bedtime, all the memories come flooding in and I cry myself to sleep every night. I torture myself with thoughts of what I am missing. Junior

27

prom at the Catholic school, the dances, walking around the city, graduating high school with my best friends. All gone in a puff of smoke.

———◇———

Daddy bought a car for his commute to work. Mom doesn't drive and I believe she doesn't want to drive. When I lived in the city, I didn't need a driver's license with buses, cabs, and my two strong legs at my beck and call. Now though, it's a 30 to 45-minute drive to visit my friends. Without the convenience of a bus or cab and being too far to walk, I don't get to be with them like before. The phone? There's one attached to the wall in the kitchen and one in the basement. So I wait in line and get pressured to hurry along my conversation. And there's no privacy. So my friendships are weakening, I can feel it.

I give myself a pep talk. *Okay, Donna, this is your life now. Move on, look ahead, stop complaining...*but everyone and everything I loved is gone. It's hard not to complain to God and to myself.

I give myself a pep talk. *Okay, Donna, this is your life now. Move on, look ahead, stop complaining.* It's all well and good to deny my grief, but everyone and everything I loved is gone. It's hard not to complain to God and to myself. I am doing the best I can but not succeeding very well.

Well, here it is February of my junior year and I've landed in the hospital for two weeks. Even as a young child, I had health problems like bronchitis and severe allergies—now it's various ailments including appendix and ovarian issues. Major surgery keeps

28

me out of school for six more weeks. Recovery is excruciating. Aspirin doesn't take away the pain of the 8-inch incision on the right side of my abdomen. Yet this pain is easier to deal with than the internal depression and grief I carry around on a daily basis. The pain of surgery will heal. I don't think my heart ever will.

Now I'm home from the hospital and thinking about returning to school. My mother comes to me and says, "Donna, you need to find a job to help pay for your medical bills." Daddy is furious, but on her insistence, I take a job as a waitress in a little restaurant down the street. I walk to and fro, several times a week. The plus is, I love the food here: hamburgers, hot dogs, fried mushrooms, milkshakes, and root beer floats. Another benefit is now I can eat in the restaurant, not at home in chaos-ville. First positive I can think of moving to Latham.

And then there's Kirk. This young and gorgeous guy comes into the restaurant frequently. He's also a really big flirt. When I see him come in, I hope with all my heart that he'll come over and sit in the center of the horseshoe counter, where I'll get to take his order. Oh, then he does. He sits down and gives me the biggest smile. I think I'm going to melt. He leans in close to me as I'm right in front of him, setting down his milkshake, hamburger, and fries. Tingling feelings creep up and down my spine, and I have butterflies in my stomach. No one has ever affected me like this. When I get off of work, Kirk is waiting for me outside to walk me home. I'm crazy about him and think about the possibility of a future together.

I have been seeing Kirk for about two months. One afternoon the phone rings and my sister answers it. "Donna, Kirk is on the phone." I race to the kitchen and Pat hands me the phone.

He says, "I have some bad news. My ex-girlfriend is pregnant and I can't see you anymore." My heart sinks into my stomach and my knees shake as I make my way to a chair at the kitchen table. The only bright spot in my life has been suddenly and shockingly snuffed out. My dream of a lifetime with Kirk is shattered. I don't know what to say so I just tell him thanks for telling me and hang up. Daddy notices my dejected look and walks over to me, gently putting his hand on my shoulder. "Okay, honey, what's wrong."

Tearing up, I say, "Daddy, Kirk just told me his ex-girlfriend is pregnant and he can't see me anymore."

"Oh, Donna, I'm so sorry. I know how much you really liked this boy. That's really tough news. I wish there was something I could do to help." God, I love my daddy. I wish he could help, but there's nothing that will take away this depression and grief, this searing pain of leaving my real life and moving to this godforsaken town. Kirk had filled me with hope and now he's gone.

Now I just have to bear it. I go to school, come home, run in the door, change clothes, walk to the restaurant to work the evening shift and walk home alone. I hate it.

Now it's been several weeks since hearing from Kirk. He stopped coming in the restaurant. I'm in my room when I hear the phone, go into the kitchen and answer it, stunned to find that it's Kirk calling me. "Donna, my ex had a miscarriage. Can I see you again?"

"I'm not sure," I tell him. "I have to talk to my dad."

How do I ask my dad if I can see him again? I go back to my room and try and sort out the swirling emotions in my head. My heart and mind seem at odds, in a way, and I'm glad I can defer this decision to my dad. I hear him opening cupboards in the kitchen and I get up to head that way.

Mustering up my courage, I approach him and say, "Daddy, Kirk called and wants to see me again. Would that be okay with you?" Daddy immediately turns around, walks over to me, and gently places his hands on my shoulders. He has the most beautiful head of black hair and the most beautiful, piercing blue eyes that look like crystal marbles. I can feel his compassion and love as he looks straight into my eyes.

"Donna, I believe every man is going to try. I also believe it's up to the girl to say no. But if you make a mistake and you get pregnant, I will be there for you. I will help you in any way I can. I trust you to do the right thing, but I will be there for you if you make a mistake."

I can't help but remember what Mom always says to me and my sisters: "If you ever get pregnant before you're married, I'll disown you."

My daddy trusts me and I vow to honor his trust in me.

> My daddy trusts me and I vow to honor his trust in me.

Kirk tries his best to get his way with me. It is REALLY DIFFICULT to stop both his insistent moves and my own burning desire—he makes me quiver from the top of my head to my toes. One day Kirk comes into the house while my parents are out. We are making out on the floor in the living room. He stands, pulls me up and, while kissing me, steers me to my parent's bedroom. He maneuvers me down to the floor. *OH NO, NO WAY, my daddy trusts me.* Breathing heavily, I gather every bit of strength within me and push him away. *Still a virgin. Sill a good Catholic girl. Still respecting Dad's trust in me.*

Several days later, I come home from work to find Aunt Lee waiting for me. She holds a newspaper page in front of me and I see Kirk, a girl, and their wedding announcement! Devastated, I am thankful he didn't have his way with me. *I will never let another boy hurt me like that again, ever!* Anger and bitterness are taking root, growing like vines that wrap around my heart and choke all the sweet life out of it, if there's any left. I don't know how to stop it, but the hardening protects my fragile emotions. *I hate this feeling. I hate my mother. I hate being so hateful. I want to love God but He's so distant.* I need help; I'm sinking into this mire and can't find my way out.

───◇───

Walking to my job at the restaurant, I always pass a quaint-looking white house with a white picket fence that surrounds it. Colorful flowers adorn the front yard from spring to fall. Occasionally I see a guy washing his car or doing odds and ends around the property.

It's the weekend and here comes the guy from the little white house. He's walking to one of the booths that's in my section. I go over to take his breakfast order, but the only thing he wants is a cup of coffee. He has his own donuts in a little brown bag. *Hmmm, peculiar.*

He begins to come into the restaurant on a regular basis and I learn his name is Dave.

"Donna," he asks, "would you like to go out with me to a drive-in movie on Saturday?"

"First, I have to ask my mother and dad if it's okay." After I take Dave to meet my parents, they approve of our date. Dave is 22, and I'm 16, and I'm feeling a bit proud of myself for dating an "older man."

Dave is newly released from the Army and suffers from trauma, one blow being the death of his father. He was in Germany when he got word of his dad's illness. Flying home, he prayed that God would keep his father alive until he got home. Unfortunately, his father died before he got to see him. After his father's death, he swore off God, and says now he's an atheist. It's nice to have a social life again, at least catching a movie here and there. But Dave is moody and drinks more than anyone I've ever been around.

After one of his alcoholic binges, I find him on the floor in the hallway of my house. He's sobbing uncontrollably about the death of his dad. Trying to hold and comfort him is very difficult. He's drunk and he's heavy. *This is a recipe for disaster.* Ignoring the signs, I continue to date him.

Doggone It!

Life for Fritzi is quite different as well. He barks at everything, can't walk me to school and he chases cars and motorcycles. He's a Beagle. He loves to run and walk with us wherever we go. The neighbors complain about his barking and running around the neighborhood. Mom does all she can to keep him calm to no avail.

The school bus stops in front of the house. It's a beautiful Spring afternoon. I walk in the door and it's quiet. Where's Fritzi? Every day he waits for us to walk in the door, tail wagging, jumping up and down excitedly to greet us. "Fritzi, Frit—zeee!" I yell, but it's quiet.

Mom sheepishly walks into the living room and says, "I know someone who has a farm and I took him there to live." I cannot believe she gave away our beloved Fritzi! I am shocked, angry, sad, and grief-stricken, but I have to get ready for work. I tuck the pain away, walk to work and try not to think about my precious, beautiful Fritzi. I tell myself, *He's happy. He's on a farm running, barking, and playing freely.* Thinking about him on the farm gives me a little comfort. I grieve for his presence and friendship. *I will never forget you, my dear, furry forever friend.*

Whenever Mom was unhappy with me about something, she would say, "If you don't behave, I'm sending you to St. Catherine's Home." St. Catherine's is an orphanage in Albany. There are days I wonder if that's where Fritzi really ended up.

Father Knows Best

It's a sunny but blistery winter day some time at the end of December 1966. Mom is up banging pots and pans around the kitchen. It's apparent she's upset about something. *Oh boy, she's in one of her rages.* I go into Mommy and Daddy's bedroom to wake Daddy up for church. He's asleep, his back to the door as I walk in. He looks so peaceful and how I hate to wake him. *How he sleeps through the banging coming from the kitchen, I'll never know.* The blankets and bedspread swallow him up to his neck and wrap him in a ball of comfort. Sunshine from the windows on the other side of the bed pours in, giving it a bright and cheery feel. I lean over and kiss him on the cheek. Slowly, he rolls over, sits up, and puts his hands on my shoulders. With sleep in his eyes, he looks at me with love and concern and says, "Donna, please don't get married too young." I hug him, smile and walk out of the room shutting the door behind me.

That's all I remember about our encounter. I only wish I had listened to his advice.

January 7, 1967, at 6:30 am, my mother is pounding on the handrail at the bottom of the stairs. She is frantic. She can't climb the stairs with the cast she is wearing from her hips to her toes. She fell over the vacuum cleaner and broke her ankle in three places a few weeks ago and had surgery to repair the damage. She's screaming, "Get up, an ambulance just left the house. Your dad's on his way to the hospital and I think he had a heart attack." *He's only 44 years old. He's had three other heart attacks and he's still here, He can't die.*

Dave comes to the house and drives me and my mother to the hospital. The nurse walks up and says, "How old are you?" When I tell her that I'm 17, she says, "I'm sorry, you can't visit your dad, the hospital rules state you must be 18 years old to visit."

I burst into tears. I cannot believe this! *I wish I lied about my age.* I am so upset. I want to see my daddy! Now two nurses are standing in front of me as if they have to block me from running down the hall to find my dad. Dave takes my hand and leads me back out to the car. All the way home all I can think about is how I didn't say goodnight to Daddy last night. I stormed upstairs because Mom and I were fighting. When I got in bed and pulled up the covers to get cozy and warm, I remembered I didn't kiss him goodnight. *I'll see him in the morning and give him a quick kiss before I start my day.* Now he's lying in the hospital and I can't tell him I love him or give him his goodnight kiss.

Crawling into bed around midnight, I pray, "Please God, let Daddy live." In the twilight before sleep, a vision appears of my daddy lying in a casket with flowers all around him. My mother is sitting in a chair at the foot of the casket resting her injured leg on a chair.

35

I'm dressed in black and I don't even own a black dress. *Oh God, please let my daddy live.* Something in me knows this isn't good.

I wake up hearing a commotion downstairs. My clock on the nightstand tells me it's 3:31 AM. I jump out of bed and run down the stairs. There's a knock at the front door, and I open it to see Uncle Lloyd, Daddy's brother. "Your mother is with your Aunt Lee," he says. "She is sedated and your aunt and grandmother are taking care of her. I am so sorry to tell you that your daddy died at 9:30 last night." Falling into a heap on the floor, I realize that my worst fears are here. *This has to be a dream, this can't be real.* I am too shocked and upset to even cry tears. I lie on the floor, curled up with my arms wrapped around my knees. I can see my uncle's shoes and then another pair of men's shoes steps in through the door. I think I'm going to throw up. Or scream. Or both.

I feel my uncle's hand gently grip my arm and pull me up off the floor. I stand and watch three more somber, silent men walk in and then close the front door. I know them. They are friends of Daddy's. My sweet Uncle Lloyd has a blank look on his face. I can tell he is in shock at the loss of his brother. They were so close as kids growing up and as adults. What a huge loss for all of us.

I am back in my bed, but I don't remember walking up here. Everything is a blur. Everything after those words, "your daddy died at 9:30 last night."

Out loud, I cry, "God, why didn't you answer my prayer?" The only thing I can think of is that God just said NO. I don't like it, don't understand why, but it's what I believe. I wanted a YES. God answered my prayer with a NO. It's done. Daddy is dead.

My daddy, my hero, my lifeline to sanity—is gone. *How are we, am I, going to live without you? I love you so much.*

Some life. I feel nothing but heartache. I'm just going through the motions as I get myself to the places I have to be. The depression deepens. I find myself sinking into depths of pain I cannot get out of. Like quicksand, I'm sinking deeper and deeper with no way out. "Help, God! I don't want to live anymore!" But I know I won't end my own life. I am the oldest of eight kids, Mom and my siblings need me to be strong to get us all through this terrible nightmare. With my heart and life in tatters, I go on.

> "Help, God! I don't want to live anymore!"

Will I ever see Daddy again? In heaven? I know this question will haunt me for many, many years to come.

———◇———

My dad's Uncle Henry suffers from severe rheumatoid arthritis. He is crippled and cannot take care of himself, so his wife quit her job and does her best to help. Grampy, my dad's father, drives over and bathes, shaves, and feeds breakfast to his brother Henry every day. It is decided that Uncle Henry will not be told about Daddy's death because his health is so fragile. We all keep the secret—but only for one day.

Sunday morning, January 8, 1967, Henry's wife walks into the bedroom. Uncle Henry opened his eyes wide, looked up at the ceiling, and said, "Okay, Donald, I'm coming." Then he took his last breath.

37

Grampy lost Donald (his precious son and my dad) and then his brother Henry, the same weekend.

Several weeks after Daddy's death, I am at Nana and Grampy's. He looks at me and says, "You know, I think your dad went to God and said, 'Uncle Henry is a burden on my dad, will you bring him up here with us?'" I don't know how things work in heaven, but it gave Grampy comfort. I cherish the time I have with him as he shares his heart.

Trying to figure out how to navigate through pain, suffering, depression, guilt, and shame is impossible. All I can do is pull this invisible plastic bubble around my mind and heart so I can't think or feel any of it. *Will I ever get out of this pit? I can't imagine things ever getting worse.* Unfortunately, I am wrong. Very, very wrong.

4

Life Without Daddy

I just woke up and for two seconds, life seemed normal. Then I remembered that Daddy is gone. Life without him is so empty and lonely. And scary. Depression and grief permeate our house. Each one of us deals with their loss in different ways. Emotionally, I feel drained of life itself, like I have no heartbeat. My little sister Lori sees someone pull our bright red station wagon into our driveway. She jumps up and down and squeals, "Daddy's home! Daddy's home!" But he doesn't walk in the front and she cries with disappointment.

Mom's a wreck. Her violent outbursts increase in frequency and intensity. Walking into her bedroom, I see her lying across her bed, cards strewn in front of her, playing solitaire. She must not be winning because she looks very, very angry. *Oh no, she's getting up off the bed.* Her face contorts into pure rage, and her light auburn-brown eyes turn black. Here comes the volcanic eruption. I move quickly to get out of her way.

Her feet hit the floor with a loud thud that rattles the walls and windows. She continues to pound her feet on the hardwood floor of the hallway and through the kitchen. Pots and pans rattle as she continues. THUMP, THUMP, THUMP through the dining room, across the living room. The pounding steps continue up the stairs to the bedrooms. I run to my room as my heart is racing in my chest and fear and terror well up in me. *Who is she going after?*

Oh my God. I hear her smacking one of my siblings. It's Cindi. I can hear the hitting, both of them yelling, and I can picture exactly what is going on since I've been in this scenario myself many times. Cindi is helpless against the onslaught of the continual, heavy-handed slaps to her head and face. I'm frozen in fear and can't do anything to help.

I don't move a muscle until I hear Mom stomp down the stairs and go back to her room. When I can catch my breath, I quietly slip upstairs to Cindi's room. She tells me that Mom lost her favorite comb and blamed her for stealing it. Cindi's face is streaming with tears and her right eye is already swollen shut from the beating.

Between her sobs that she is trying to swallow so Mom won't hear, she tells me that when Mom paused a moment after five straight minutes of assaulting her own daughter, she reached to the back of her head—Lo and behold, she found her missing comb tucked in her hair right where she left it. She snickered when she realized her mistake, and without an apology, she walked out to head back downstairs.

Now I'm in bed, but there's no way I can fall asleep with my heart still racing and so many emotions flooding me. Guilt-ridden, I'm still full of fear. I did nothing to help my sister. Hatred for my mother overtakes all other feelings. *I would love to beat the hell out of that horrible woman. What a terrible thought. How disgusting you are Donna to think like this.* My mind is in a battle to keep sane or to commit my own act of violence.

My anger and fear are lessening just enough that I just might be able to fall asleep. I'm emotionally exhausted, that's for sure. I close my eyes and tears streak my cheeks and onto my pillow.

After work, I walk into Mom's bedroom, and she is lying on her side, sprawled across the bed. She has dozens of family pictures fanned out and in piles on top of the bedspread. She stares at me with a menacing grin. *She is daring me to cry or react in some way.* I don't know what to do. She will not allow me to grieve. I see it in her eyes. All I can think of is the wicked witch from *Wizard of Oz.* Mom's look says, "Go ahead, go ahead and cry and see what will happen to you if you do, my little pretty, ha-ha-ha." Completely intimidated, I leave her room and find something else to keep me occupied.

In bed at night, I grieve for my dad. My hero, my daddy is gone and there's no one to help me through the intense pain that continually grips my heart and mind. Daddy gave me compassion, mercy and understanding. Whatever my problem or hurt, he would sit with me, listen, and help me figure things out. There was such caring and trust between us. *Oh my God, I miss him so much. Life will never be the same without him.*

My 18th birthday is here, and I'm met with my birthday surprise from Mom. "Donna, you're 18 now, and I'll no longer get your dad's Social Security benefits for you. I want $50.00 a month for rent, or you need to get your own place to live." Stunned is an understatement of how I feel.

Right after graduation I start working as a claims clerk in an insurance company. Entry level clerks like me don't make a lot of money. Resentment wells up within me. *I had to give her money to help pay for my surgery and now I have to give her rent. I drive to work with a friend since I can't drive. What do I do, who can I turn to now?*

I'm hopelessly lost. Daddy always took care of me. I feel like a little kid being thrown out on the street. Maybe I'll run off to St. Catherine's Home.

A Way Out

The afternoon of Christmas Day, 1967, Dave and I are headed with his family. After dinner we gather together in the living room to exchange gifts. Without warning, Dave is down on one knee reaching into his pocket. He's opening up a little blue box. It's a small but beautiful solitaire diamond ring. "Donna, will you marry me?"

"Yes, I will." His family is overjoyed and claps with glee as he slips the ring onto my finger. My emotions are in turmoil as I look at this ring and the man I just agreed to marry. *I'm getting out of my mother's house* is, unfortunately, my most positive thought. But I worry: *I'm a virgin. I've never had sex before. Can I endure having sex with Dave?* I remember how I felt when I was with Kirk. My heart raced, I had butterflies in my stomach and chills up and down my spine when he touched me. I don't feel ANY of these things with Dave. Yet... *I need to get out of my mother's house. Dave is my way out. Let's do this.*

My savings account is growing as I put my little paycheck into the bank, minus $50.00 of course. My savings are enough to pay for a nice wedding. Everything is arranged. Dave and I met with the priest at the Catholic church. He is not Catholic, but agrees to raise our kids in the Catholic faith.

The wedding day is here. My house is all aflutter with activity. All of us getting ready for the special occasion. The photographer arrives and begins taking pictures. All of my attendants look gorgeous in their multi-colored dresses. My white wedding gown has a large hoop underneath it giving it a swooping feel as I walk. The limousine is here and we're on our way to the Catholic church in Albany.

Uncle Lloyd is giving me away. *Why is he crying?* As we walk down the aisle, I see my mother, Nana, and Grampy, all with tears. *Why are they all crying? It's my wedding day…Maybe they think I'm making a huge mistake…*

Well, I definitely know how to hide my feelings, so I make a smiling face and put one foot in front of the other. But inside I'm screaming. *What am I doing?! I can't go through with this. I don't want to do this. I'm MARRYING Dave? I can't even imagine having sex with him.* And here I am, at the altar. "I do." I am now married to Dave.

Daddy's voice echoes in my head, "Donna, please don't get married too young." How I wish I had listened to his wise words.

"Donna, please don't get married too young."

Period number two—missed. I'm certain I'm pregnant…and I am excited! Dave walks in from work. I say to him, "Please sit down, I have something to tell you."

"What?" he asks, looking concerned, of course.

"I'm pregnant. We're going to have a baby!" I'm so excited at the prospect of being a mom. He looks at me with a completely blank face, says, "Great," and walks away. He just ripped the joy out of my heart. Dave and I are going to be parents! Why isn't he as ecstatic about having a baby as I am? Maybe having a baby will help our marriage.

It's Saturday night. Friends are here, and we're having our usual weekend get-together. Dave is drunk and acting quite belligerent, spewing sarcastic remarks and nasty comments at me in front of our guests. Disgusted with his behavior, my cup of now cold coffee lands in his lap—after I throw it at him.

Neither Dave nor our friends seem to react at all. Through this whole scenario, we keep playing cards like nothing happened. The night ends, our company is gone, and suddenly Dave throws up all over the kitchen floor. I keep my mouth shut, but I'm thinking, *Why can't you use the bathroom, you jerk.* Wiping up vomit that smells like alcohol is disgusting. And it's hard to maneuver myself to kneel on the floor because of my big pregnant belly. I clean up the mess and try to get the smell off of the floor, out of the apartment, and off of me.

YIKES…a sharp pain hits my belly. This can't be happening. Dave's drunk. *How am I going to get to the hospital? Who can I call?* I lie down in bed and wait for the mild contractions to either escalate or stop. Finally, contractions stop. "We're okay," I say to my baby.

It's my 20th birthday. Tricia Jean, our beautiful 6 lb. 6 oz. baby girl is born at 4:30 a.m. The nurse comes in and places her in my arms. Love pours out of me for this precious little miracle. This is by far the best birthday present I've ever had.

Help! I don't know the first thing about taking care of a baby. I'm tired, depressed, and lonely. Dave is unemotionally available. He works, comes home, eats, watches TV, then goes to bed. Every weekend he's drunk. I'm convinced most of it is my fault. And I don't feel like I can ask my mom for any help. Why subject myself to her probable answer of "no." Resentment and bitterness churn within me towards him. I feel like I married my mother, without the physical abuse.

Now I feel a little better, but not because it's any easier with Tricia, who is now six months old. I find out I am expecting baby number two. I love being pregnant and the feel of a precious baby inside me.

A few days after Christmas in 1970, our wonderful 7 lb. 2 oz. baby boy is born. The nurse comes in and places him in my arms. He nuzzles his head into the corner of my arm as close to me as he can get. After my daddy, he is named Donald Joseph. Several months later, baby number three is on the way.

Tami is born in the summer of 1972, weighing in at 5 lb. 12 oz. She's a little peanut. Her weight drops to 5 lb. 5 oz. and she won't eat. The pediatrician says, "We are concerned because she is not eating. We're keeping her an extra day." My doctor discharges me and I'm sent home without my baby. My heart is heavy, hating to go home without her in my arms. The following day I'm overjoyed as we're on our way to pick her up and bring her home. Fortunately, she begins to eat and gain weight.

My children are HUGE blessings in my life. All three are full of energy and mischief. I don't know how to discipline properly. I yell and pound my feet to no avail. No matter how hard I try, I can't protect them from some sort of trouble. Donald falls down while he has a part to the vacuum cleaner in his mouth which slices his tonsil in half. One day he decides to climb up the front of our chest of drawers where the TV is, trying to turn the channel. The dresser tips over on top of him. Fortunately, he isn't hurt when the tip of the dresser lands on the corner edge of the mattress. *I wish I knew how to be a better mom.* My biggest fear is becoming like my mother.

Donald especially has many freak accidents I can't explain. Falling over the fence hanging upside down by the cuff of his pants. Getting his leg stuck behind the radiator. One time he's jumping on the bed and I calmly said, "Donald, that's not a good idea." Just then, he stops going up and down and looks like he's been jerked sideways across the room. He landed on a small metal box located on the floor between the wall and the smaller dresser. The sound of his nose hitting that metal box sends shivers down my spine. *Oh my God, what's happening to my son!* Horrified, I pick him up and see he has two black eyes. Rushing him immediately to the E.R., doctors and nurses seem not to believe my story. I wouldn't have believed it if I hadn't seen it with my own eyes. It's so hard to be looked upon as the same type of abuser as my mother. Everything in me tries to avoid being her. Am I perfect? No, but I try with all my heart to protect my little ones. If I only had the answer to how this is happening to my kids maybe I could stop it somehow.

At age 23 I feel like I'm 80 years old. Dave and I are not in a good place in our marriage. I want a caring man like my daddy in my life. A husband to love me the way Daddy loved Mom. *Why is he so much like my mom? He doesn't beat me, thank God for that.* He's a good provider, but he's sarcastic, angry, and an abusive drunk. I'm pretty angry myself. Nothing he does is good enough. My heart is totally shut down. My kids are my life and I love them with everything in me. Dave is another story.

Depression, fatigue, and unresolved bitterness drain the life out of me. All I want to do is watch soap operas, eat cookies, and sleep. It's too painful to be present to the life I find myself in. Even with no outside job, it's incredibly hard to take care of the house, cook, and care for three little kids. My numerous health problems add to my stress; serious female issues, surgeries, back problems, viruses, and pneumonia, on top of the emotional issues, complicate my life even further.

> My kids are my life and I love them with everything in me. Dave is another story.

My favorite soap operas fill my days. *What if I meet someone and have an affair like Erica Kane on "All My Children?" She has one man after another in her bed.* My mind starts to wander. I become addicted to romance and pornography: books, magazines, and movies of a faceless lover who rescues me from all of life's pain and misery fill my mind as I satisfy myself sexually apart from my husband. My imagination runs wild. I don't need a man to give me an orgasm. *I'll take care of myself. I've been doing this since I was four years old anyway.*

The carpenter is here to give an estimate on a room we want remodeled. My hair is a mess, the house is a disaster, and my kids are playing rambunctiously in the living room. *He is gorgeous.* Showing him the room we want remodeled, he begins taking measurements and I run downstairs to put on a pot of coffee.

He's done. He's walking towards me. Oh, my heart is racing. He looks at me and says, "Could I have a cup of coffee?" giving me a flirty wink and a smile. Quickly two cups of coffee are on the kitchen table.

We've been sitting here for two hours. Getting up to leave, he turns to me, touches my cheek, and says, "I have to come back tomorrow to finish up my estimate. Is that okay?"

"Of course, I'll be home all day."

Uh oh, he's very attentive looking me in the eye as he carries on about what, I don't remember. I love the attention, the conversation, and the feeling of someone being interested in me as a person. I'm in BIG trouble. This is not good. I love the attention and can't wait to see him tomorrow.

It's early and Bruce is coming to finish up the estimate. Jumping in the shower, I want to smell and look beautiful. Eye shadow, foundation and a little lipstick, there. A little vacuuming, dusting and picking up the toys makes the house a little more presentable then yesterday. The kids are in for a nap. Coffee is brewing and so am I.

Bruce is here and says, "HI beautiful, you look gorgeous today."

"Thank you." Running upstairs, he finishes the estimate rather quickly. Waiting patiently in the kitchen, I hear him coming down. Turning the corner, he walks into the kitchen and I offer him a cup of coffee and a seat at the table. Sitting down next to me, we stare into each other's eyes. Our conversations are deep as we share about our lives. Empathy pours out of him as he's listening intently to my story of abuse and loss. My desire for intimacy and caring attention from a man is being fulfilled right here in my kitchen. *My God, I don't even have to leave the house to have an affair, it's right here at my front door.* A carpenter shows up and I'm undone.

Dave and the kids are sleeping. I leave and go visit my best friend, Ro. Several nights a week we get together at her house. We commiserate about life, pour over catalogs and make out our wish lists.

Bruce's wife is out of town and he invites me over to his place. Like picking petals off a daisy, the battle is on. I will go, I will not go. The "I will go" wins. I say I'm going over to my girlfriend's and drive to Bruce's. *My God, what am I doing? How can I do this to my husband?* After several months of flirting and exchanging passionate kisses, we consummate our affair.

The guilt and shame overwhelm me. Walking into my bedroom, I awaken Dave and have sex with him. I feel sick. I'm obsessed with Bruce but to relieve the guilt and shame, I have sex with my husband. *Well, that didn't work! What kind of woman does this?* I hate myself. I'm in trouble. This is not going to end well. *Bruce loves me. Dave and I will get a divorce, and I can be with Bruce as soon as he's divorced.*

If something seems too good to be true, it's not real. Soon after Bruce and I consummate our "love" affair, he ends it. *What was this to him? Was I a challenge, a toy to be played with?* Anger, bitterness, and depression rage within me. There's nowhere to go, no one to talk to.

Tasting what it's like to be with someone who makes me feel loved, I'm now on a quest to find a guy like my dad. Dave and I agree to separate, although we live in the same house until he can find a place to live. Sometimes I leave Dave with the kids and I go out to the bars with my friends for some fun.

Dave needs a wife who loves him more than I do. I think we need marriage counseling or a divorce or something. This is not normal. I need to confess to my priest and find out how to stop this life of sin. How can I possibly save my marriage and confess to Dave what I've done? I honestly think he'll kill me if he knows the truth.

The appointment with my priest is very disappointing. "Father, I have a sin problem. I want to have sex with men other than my husband. I go to the bars without him. I want to go home with anyone who shows me attention."

He says, "Well, I go to the bars, and I don't have that problem. You should be able to enjoy your time there like I do." *REALLY?????* I can't believe my ears. He recommends divorce because Dave is not Catholic. *What kind of priest are you?*

My neighbor knocks on the front door. I ask Karen to come on in. After some small talk, I tell her the priest recommended Dave and I divorce. She takes a deep breath and says, "I don't know, Donna, if you should listen to the priest. I work at the Holiday Inn across the street from the Catholic church. The priests come over to the hotel with flowers and wine, get a room, then entertain the village prostitutes."

"Are you KIDDING me?" I cry out. "No wonder I can't get any help from the priest. He's sleeping with prostitutes and doesn't consider it a problem?"

After Karen leaves to go home, I yell at the ceiling, "God, I've done it your way all my life, now I'm gonna do it my way! You need to show me yourself what's right and what's wrong." Desperately looking for answers to my sin problem, hopelessness overwhelms me. The church sickens me…at least, the priests.

I'm done with the Catholic church and the Catholic faith." At 24 years old, I'm on a quest to find real love, to find a man who will treat me like my daddy did. Get out of my way world—here I come.

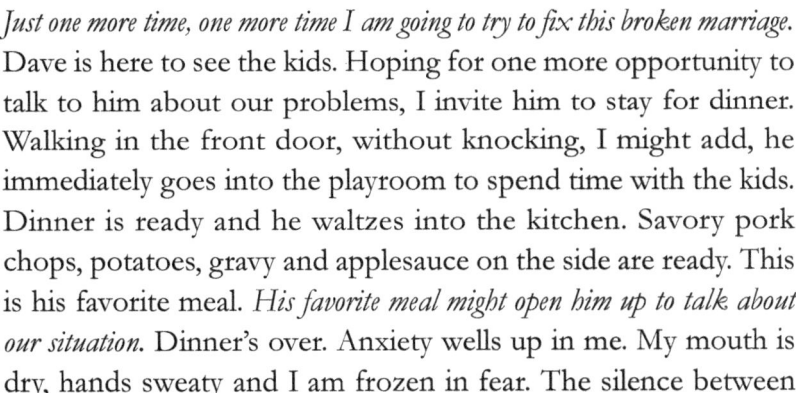

Just one more time, one more time I am going to try to fix this broken marriage. Dave is here to see the kids. Hoping for one more opportunity to talk to him about our problems, I invite him to stay for dinner. Walking in the front door, without knocking, I might add, he immediately goes into the playroom to spend time with the kids. Dinner is ready and he waltzes into the kitchen. Savory pork chops, potatoes, gravy and applesauce on the side are ready. This is his favorite meal. *His favorite meal might open him up to talk about our situation.* Dinner's over. Anxiety wells up in me. My mouth is dry, hands sweaty and I am frozen in fear. The silence between us is deafening.

He's getting up from the table. Without giving me a second look, he hugs the kids, turns around, and walks out the door. Not a thank you, nothing, not one word. *ARE YOU KIDDING ME?* You come in here, eat dinner, leave me with the cleanup, and walk out. *YOU JERK!* At this point, I know my marriage is over. I have no way of fixing this mess I've gotten myself into.

Oblivious to the disaster on the horizon, I feel like I'm standing on the edge of a cliff. I keep having this dream over and over: I'm free falling, falling, falling yet never hitting bottom and with a jolt, I wake up. I think my dream means my life is crashing. There seems to be no way of stopping this downward spiral. *I need something, someone to rescue me.* This voice in my head runs constantly in my brain—*Keep looking for Mr. Right, Donna. He's out there somewhere. One*

51

day, you'll find a man just like your daddy and he'll take good care of you. I can only hope this is true. *I want my daddy…*

Divorce May Create More Problems than It Solves

My sister Debby and I walk into divorce court. Dave is sitting on one side of the room and I'm on the other. Our divorce is granted the day after my 24th birthday. The judge finds it in his heart to award me $100.00 a month. What a joke. This is just enough to cover my mortgage payment. He didn't even consider insurance, utilities, the car payment, and child support. My children are 7, 6, and 4 and I'm awarded full custody. This is good for my heart, but how can I support us?

Feeling guilty for being the "cheater" I've decided not to fight the judgment. Even though I know Dave is seeing another woman, I truly believe I'm the only one guilty. A month later, Dave and his girlfriend are married. *He sure played on my guilt.*

Child care is very expensive. I began receiving Welfare and Food Stamps to help supplement my expenses. Budgeting and writing checks are not my forte. Bills keep piling up and buying clothes and food for my kids is darn near impossible.

A local band in the area is looking for a female singer. A guy I started seeing encouraged me to audition. Walking into the gym where the audition is being held, my stage fright is out of control. My heart is racing faster than the tune "Wipe Out." My hands are sweaty and I'm terrified. Amplifiers, sound equipment and microphones are placed strategically about the stage. This is the first time ever singing solo for anyone. My own mother never heard me sing. Sure, I was in several musical performances in the Catholic school—hiding in the back row, singing with others drowning out my voice because I wasn't good enough for a solo part.

The head of the group walks over and hands me a piece of sheet music. "Angel Baby" is the song and I've never heard it before. Graciously, the band works with me to learn it quickly. With everything in me, I hit the high note on key. Much to my immense surprise, I'm now the female singer in a band called "Skippy and the Pistons."

> Much to my immense surprise, I'm now the female singer in a band called "Skippy and the Pistons."

All I need now are babysitters to take care of the kids while I go with the band to rehearsal and perform at weddings and various clubs around the area.

Several teenagers live in my neighborhood. After my divorce, they visit me regularly just to hang out. With several younger siblings, I find this quite normal. They're like my family.

Denise is moving in so she can babysit and help with stuff around the house. She lives in a very dysfunctional home and we're helping each other out. She reminds me of my younger sister, and I feel pretty good about leaving my kids in her care. Denise has several friends who start hanging around the house. Several stay overnight and help out. There's a girl who's in her early twenties and I am at ease because she's a bit older and hopefully more mature. Having an adult around gives me a sense of assurance about my kids' safety and care when I'm working.

One afternoon a Case Worker from Welfare shows up at my front door. Inviting her in, she looks around the house, makes her way to the kitchen and sits down. "I'm here to inform you we are going to take your house if you don't get a job, a real job." *You've got to be kidding!* Working with the band doesn't pay well. Welfare and food stamps are a great help financially. Where can I find a job making enough money to support my kids and pay for child care? Stripped of welfare and food stamps, I'm not sure how to keep from losing my house and my mind at the same time. *This really sucks.*

Losing government assistance causes a huge financial burden. Paying mortgage, insurance, utilities, gas for the car, feeding and clothing my kids feels impossible. To get more income from Dave, I'll have to go back to court. With no money to hire an attorney, I'm stuck.

There's this detective I know at our local police station. He dated a good friend of mine. He and I became friends, although we never dated. One evening he stops in for a visit. Escorting him into the living room, he sits down on the couch. "This is not a social visit, Donna." Nausea hits my stomach as fear and anxiety rise up within me. *What is he thinking? Is he here to take my kids?*

"We are watching your house very closely. You have young kids hanging around here all the time. If they hide any drugs in your house, you're the one going to jail because you're the adult. It doesn't matter if you know there's drugs or not. If we find them, you're in big trouble."

"Oh my God, Ron. As far as I know, they don't have any drugs here." In all seriousness, I never searched to see if there were any drugs stashed somewhere. *Better start looking as soon as possible. Jail is the last place I want to end up.* Ron stands up, gives me a friendly hug, and looks at me with empathy and concern. "Donna, seriously, you need to search the house right after I leave. Trouble from law enforcement is the last thing you need."

"Honest Ron, I promise to search every area I can think of. Last thing I want is to go to jail." When he leaves, I begin hunting everywhere and searching through every crack and crevice. Fortunately, I find no drugs. Although we've smoked marijuana together here many times, I never thought they would stash it in my home. *Thank God for one small miracle. At least I can stay out of jail for a little while at least. What else can go wrong???*

Medication Sensitivity

This pulled muscle in my back is excruciating. The E.R. doctor prescribes 10 mg. of Valium. Taking the medication, I decide to go to my bed and rest. YIKES—this black bat is swinging over my bed. It has great big green eyes and looks like a HUGE fly. Hell, it's falling—it's on my stomach. I grab it around the neck and start thrashing it around to get it off my body. In the midst of wrestling this awful creature, I begin to wake up to my actual surroundings. What?? What am I doing? To my horror, my hands are wrapped around the throat of my precious cat, Cuddles. I'm shaking the living daylights out of him. It's not a bat, it's my cat!!! Thank God…I could have killed my precious fur baby.

Stupid me! What were you thinking Donna? You can't even take an aspirin or Excedrin without getting sick. Medications, alcohol, and environmental changes are detrimental to my health, almost fatal. Asthma, brain fog, and passing out have sent me to the emergency room more than once. *You need to be more careful, Donna.* No more Valium for this girl.

Another Fine Mess You've Gotten Me Into

Several of us are at the local bar dancing and partying. This guy, Adam, is walking over. "Hi, will you dance with me?"

"Sure, I'd love to." He can really dance and he's really cute.

Our relationship develops quickly. We are going to move to Florida with my kids and get married. This is my newest escape plan. The police are watching my house. My mom is a widow with five kids at home and she doesn't have the energy or patience to help me. Moving to Florida seems to be my only recourse.

My phone is ringing, picking it up, oh no, it's my mother. "Donna, I need to talk to you. Come over and have dinner tomorrow night so we can talk." *Uh oh, I'm in trouble. What does she want? Maybe she'll offer to let me stay with her for a while.* Thinking about moving to Florida is causing me anxiety. *Where will we live? How can I afford to take care of my kids? What do I do with the house? Adam is great, but I don't know him very well. Should we get married? Restlessness and unease cause sleepless nights and worrisome days.*

My heart is thumping out of my chest as I walk into my mother's house. *What does she want? Am I in for a lecture about how bad I am? How stupid I am? STOP IT DONNA. Let the negative voices go. STOP.*

My mother is sitting at her dining room table with my precious aunt, her sister. "Donna, come in here and sit with us." *Uh oh, here it comes.* My blood pressure is rising by the minute. My heart and head start pounding as fear of her wells up inside me. *Will I ever get over these feelings with her?*

"We know how tired you are, Donna. You've been through so much with the divorce and so much sickness. We think you should rent out your house. Ask Dave and his wife to take the kids on a temporary basis. Go to Florida, set up housekeeping, get married. Then bring the kids down there after you have everything settled. By then, they'll be out of school for the summer, and the transition will be easier for them."

There's silence between us. "I'll think about it," is all I can say. This is a very difficult decision and one I can't make lightly.

This is not at all what I expected from either of them. *Ask Dave to take the kids? Go to Florida without my kids?* This is devastating... *what choice do I have? I'm in trouble here. She can toss my kids away like she did Fritzi? If I ask Dave to take the kids, aren't I abandoning them like she did to my precious dog? I'm so confused.*

After spending days contemplating all my options, I've decided to follow their advice. *What choice do I have?* All I can do is hope this works out according to plan.

Dave is here. We begin loading clothes, toys, and other non-essentials for him to take with him. I wish I could sense what my kids are feeling right now. *I cannot believe this is happening. My kids are going to live with Dave and his wife.* Oh my GOD, I'm sick. I don't want this. My heart feels like it's being cut out of my chest and I feel every bit of the pain associated with it. Every slice of the blade, piercing my heart, into the core of my being. How do I say goodbye to my precious children? I love them so much. *I don't think I can, I don't think I want to live through this.* Something tells me, this is not going to end well, not one bit.

This must be it. I double-check the paper with the address Adam sent me. SERIOUSLY??? I can't believe my eyes. YOU'VE GOT TO BE KIDDING ME! What is this place? This doesn't look like a place he came here to set up for me and the kids. Pushing the door open, I feel it hit something. Adam? He's sound asleep on a mattress. It's on the floor and pushed up into a corner against the wall. This isn't even a bedroom. It's a small area about 4'x4'. There are four other guys sprawled around various cubby holes in this boarding house. This place is FILTHY. It's like walking into a pigpen. The smell of alcohol, vomit, and sweat hits my nose. It's disgusting. "Adam, wake up."

"Huh, what? Oh God, you're here."

With a smart reply all I can say is, "Yup, I'm here. I'm exhausted and need sleep and some food. The bus ride all the way from New York was long and uncomfortable. The cab ride here wasn't a piece of cake either." *Oh my God how am I going to sleep on that mattress? Are there any spiders or bugs under those dirty sheets?* Wow, I must be tired to even be thinking about laying down on that mattress. With great trepidation for fear of bugs, spiders and snakes, oh my, I crawl onto the mattress. No need to change my clothes. I hope I can sleep. I'm beyond exhausted.

Dreams of Tricia, Donald, and Tami torment me and keep me from deep sleep. I clearly hear, "Mommy, Mommy where are you?" I see Tami banging on the car window as she's driving away with her dad. I bolt upright, with my eyes stinging from the tears welling up from this nightmare…Crap, I give up. This is so frustrating. My eyes open slightly and focus on the window at the end of the mattress. "WHAT THE HECK IS THAT!!?" I scream at the top of my lungs. Adam and three guys come running over to me.

"What's the matter, are you okay?" asks Adam, thinking I've been attacked by some murderous intruder.

"No, I'm not ok. That's the BIGGEST DAMN BUG I'VE EVER SEEN and IT FLIES. What is it?"

"Oh, that. It's a palmetto bug…he won't hurt you."

"The hell he won't." My terror and fear of any kind of bug triples at the sight of this monster. Thankfully, Adam gets rid of the critter. My fears are not alleviated. There has to be another around here somewhere. Where there's one, there's more.

"Give me that newspaper." Rolling it up, my sleeping now consists of one eye open, the other eye shut. If another one shows up here it's dead, dead, dead. The problem is, I wish I were dead. What in the world have I done?

Geo and I became friends when he started coming to my house with Adam. Geo hangs with us here quite frequently. He lives in New York during the summer months. During the winter months, he resides here in Florida. He moved here shortly before I arrived. He's Cuban, a bit older, probably in his mid-thirties. He's gay. He says he goes both ways. He's extremely handsome and very masculine. He doesn't look gay. What does a gay person look like anyway?

To Hell and Back

A lot of our time is spent taking on odd jobs here and there. Sambos Restaurant is the place I work a few days a week to help with some of the expenses. The guys sell their blood so we can buy a loaf of bread and some peanut butter and jelly for sandwiches.

This particular day we went into a bar for a drink. My tip money from Sambos came in handy. The lights are low with a yellowish hue, and one bare lightbulb hangs down over the bar. It feels creepy and I don't like how dark it is. I don't like the vibe here at all. Feels suffocating. Stay calm, Donna. Don't panic.

The Black Russian with a double shot of vodka is beginning to have its intended effect. Calming down, panic subsiding, I look over and see Adam talking to some guy I've never seen before. Taking another sip of my drink, Adam turns and comes walking over towards me. He takes a couple of tokes off the joint he's holding then hands it to me. "What's this?" I know what marijuana is, this just looks different.

"It's just weed, it won't hurt you, just helps you relax." Drinking and tokes on the joint help numb my pain. I'm so tired of the hurt, the guilt, and the horror of leaving my kids. All I do is cry or think about ways to kill myself that won't mean suffering, like throwing myself in front of a bus or train.

Something about my intoxication feels very different than anything I've experienced before. What's happening to me? The place is swimming around me. I feel like I'm about to lose that peanut butter and jelly sandwich. *This is stupid. You know how sensitive you are to drugs and chemicals. I don't care. Let me pass out right here.*

> Something about my intoxication feels very different than anything I've experienced before. What's happening to me?

The stranger Adam talked to earlier is walking towards me. What's he doing? He picks me up off the barstool. He's carrying me out of the bar to the parking lot. He's putting me on a blanket in the back of his van. I can barely comprehend what's happening, but can't move my body.

Oh God, he's getting in and starting the van. *Where are we going?*
Where are we? We're stopped. The back van door starts to open.
Panic permeates the thick fog of being high and numb. Is he going
to kill me and leave me somewhere? Terror fills my mind but I can't
react. Feeling sick, limp, and lifeless, I'm carried into a motel room.
Like a sack of potatoes, I'm thrown onto the bed. I hear the door
open and close. He's gone. And then…only blackness.

What, in Hell??

HELP, GOD! Don't leave me here. Oh my God, Jesus, help me.
Flames are shooting up through my torso. Internal fire, torment,
screams. HELP, GOD, JESUS DON'T LET ME DIE. JESUS,
DON'T LEAVE ME HERE. HELP, GOD! This torture is
unbearable. I don't want to stay here forever. Oh God, Jesus,
stop this. Will this ever end?

Suddenly, peace, no more fire, torment or suffering. Beginning to
rouse I open my eyes. Geo's here sitting on the floor next to my
bed. What's going on? Sweat's pouring down his face, his hands
are wet and clammy. He looks at me and says, "I couldn't find a
pulse. You weren't breathing. I didn't think you were gonna make
it. It took me 45 minutes to get you back."

I can barely speak but I manage to say, "Thank you, Geo. You saved
my life. Thank you, thank you so much…Geo, what happened?"

"I was pulling into the parking lot of the bar when I saw that
guy carrying you to his van," Geo says. "I couldn't get to you
fast enough so I followed the van and rushed in after he pulled
away. I found you here on the bed and you weren't breathing.
I immediately started CPR. Honestly, I was terrified you weren't

going to make it but I'm so glad you did." I look around and see Adam and a few other guys passed out around the room.

Looking back at Geo I say, "Thank you Geo, you saved my life. I owe you so much, thank you, thank you. How can I ever repay you?" Still groggy from the drugs, alcohol and sheer exhaustion, I fall back to sleep.

We all leave the hotel the next day and travel around the area. I quit Sambos to work at a restaurant in Frog City. We sleep in the restaurant on the concrete floor. Realizing that Adam has no intention of marrying me or setting up a home for me and my kids, I save up my tip money and hop on a bus back to New York.

Home Again

My desire to die left me quickly after my near-death experience. I head to my home where I lived before my ill-fated escape to Florida. The door to my house is unlocked. As I walk inside, shock and disgust at the mess I see is unbelievable. What in the world happened? It's early March, 20-degree temperatures, the house is freezing and so am I. One of my neighbors shows up at the front door. "Your renters moved out in January. Next thing the fire department shows up and has to pump water out of your basement. All your radiators and pipes froze, burst and water gushed all through the house." Every pipe and radiator in the house have cracks in them from water damage. The hardwood floors are wet and buckled up in various places throughout. The smell of mold and mildew fill the air. My insurance expired and nothing is covered. What a crazy mess. My house isn't paid for, it's uninhabitable, no insurance to pay for it, and I'm broke. *What do I do now? Where can I go?* This is another hell of a mess you've gotten yourself into Donna.

My mother lets me stay with her until I find somewhere to live. Of course, it's $50 a month rent to live in a small bedroom. Negative thoughts flood my mind and won't shut up. *What a failure you are Donna. You failed before Florida, you failed in Florida, and now your house is in shambles. What a disgrace you are to your family and everyone around you.* Depression, fear, my mother's words "you're stupid, you can't do anything right, you'll never amount to anything you little hussy" keep me in a paralyzed state, like the deer in the headlights. All I want to do is sleep in this dark bedroom and avoid everything and everyone.

My mother comes into the room where I'm sleeping. "Donna, wake up, this came for you today."

"What is it?" I ask.

"It's a summons."

I open the letter in disbelief. "You've got to be kidding me! Dave is taking me to court for permanent custody of the kids. This isn't what we planned. It was supposed to be temporary!" I am outraged! He broke our deal. My mother just looks at me, turns, and walks out of the room.

The courtroom looks like it was painted around 1930 in this awful dark green. The judge is sitting at his big mahogany desk in the front of the room. Dave is sitting with his wife at a table across the room. Seated with him is his lawyer. By myself, I'm sitting at a table across from Dave. The judge hears both sides of the story and decides he wants me to have custody. *Oh, if only that could work.*

And then I say the hardest two words I've ever had to say in my life. "I can't." Everyone stares at me.

"Judge," I go on, "I have nowhere to go. My house is wrecked I don't have a job or a car. How can I support three little kids when I can't even take care of myself?" I voluntarily relinquish custody of my three beautiful kids. Their welfare is at stake. I'm no good for them. They're better off without me. My mother doesn't want the responsibility of me and my kids. Who can blame her? She has five kids at home, and she's worn out. The decision is made. Dave and his wife now have full, permanent custody. Shame overwhelms my heart and mind.

This is best for my kids, I tell myself. They are in a stable environment now. They will eat properly, be in the same school system, and have a roof over their heads. Most of all, they'll have two parents to take care of them. *Their mother is stupid and a failure. They don't need me anyway.*

The proceedings are over. Walking into the Women's restroom, I crumble into a heap on the floor. Sobbing uncontrollably, rocking back and forth, I scream softly into my coat so nobody can hear me, TRICIA, DONALD, TAMI....OH GOD I LOVE YOU, I'M SO SORRY!!! This arrangement was never supposed to be permanent. Not in my mind. Not ever.

Several days later, one of my sisters is yelling, "Hey Donna, Geo's on the phone for you."

"Hi, Geo, how are you?" I ask.

"Great, I'm coming up to New York. I want to buy your house. I'll pay for the balance of the mortgage and any other expenses associated with it." He lets me know he's heard about its current condition and figured I'd be eager to get rid of it.

"Geo! Oh my God, that will take care of everything. Of course, it's yours. The least I can do is sell you my house. Geo, you saved my life and I'm so thankful and I will never forget it." I won't make a profit, but he saved my life so it's the least I can do for him.

Geo offers me a room at what is now his house. He says he wants to marry me. "Geo, I love you, but I could never compete with your boyfriends. I'm honored you would want to marry me, but it will never work between us." We decided a mutual friendship rather than a romantic relationship is best for both of us.

Living with my mother put me back in "little girl mode." I feel completely powerless around her. Her berating, scoldings and controlling behavior drives me to the brink of insanity. Maybe I'm over the brink, if anything, I'm pretty close to it. My green garbage bag is packed with all my earthly goods. Geo is here and we're headed to his place—my old run-down house.

It's freezing cold in here and we have no running water. Geo put a generator in the basement to help keep the house somewhat warm. It's still March and the temperatures are downright frigid. He's carrying a bucket of warm water up to my room so I can wash up and not freeze to death. I look in the mirror and imagine icicles hanging off my nose—not very attractive.

Many of Geo's gay friends come to visit regularly. We have dinner parties, go dancing at various straight and gay clubs around the area. These men are some of the most respectful I've ever been around. It's such a shame not one of them is interested in me. They're crazy about Geo. Still, I'm not comfortable as the only female with so many men around all the time. And I'm sick of shivering with cold. I guess I'll move back to Mom's for a while.

Starting Over

The pain of relinquishing custody of my children is too much to bear. I don't want to live. The despair is gut wrenching. *Come on Donna, you've got to get out of this depression. GET UP! MOVE!* Just then my sister Cindi knocks on my bedroom door and walks in. She tells me she knows of this little bar in the area and they need a waitress. I get my butt out of bed and go up there to put in my application. I'm hired on the spot and asked to start work that night. I barely feel up to it, but gather my strength and take this one first step out of my dark place.

A friend of mine has a trailer he's renting out. I decide to leave my mother's and move in a few days later. It's awesome for one reason and one reason only: My mother doesn't live here—I have the place to myself.

On weekends, a country band performs at the bar where I work. During one of their rehearsals, I learn they want another female singer. *Hmmm…I wonder?* Walking up to Johnny, the drummer and band leader, I say, "Hey Johnny, would it be okay if I auditioned? I don't know any country songs, but I'm willing to learn."

"Sure, come on up, let's hear what you got."

Country music is not my favorite genre but singing anything on stage is better than waiting tables and serving drinks all night. *Okay, Dolly Parton, I'm gonna give you a run for your money. Here we go.* I try with all my heart to sing "I'm Not Lisa" and "Delta Dawn." Johnny hires me and promises to add more tunes other than country to the sets. My desire is to sing a variety of music. I love

Barbara Streisand and the BeeGees, but Johnny has no desire to learn anything other than country so that's what I'm stuck with for now.

I hear of an opportunity and audition with a more musically wide-ranging band and start working with them. Our band, Freestyle, is very successful. Ray Batcher is a phenomenal lead singer and guitar player. Everywhere we play, we pack in crowds eager to hear a 50s/60s set, a Country Rock set, and a Disco set. Ray is so versatile in everything he plays. His brother, David, is very gifted as are all our talented musicians. My piano skills are okay but not band quality. I'm really great on the tambourine, have some good dance moves, and above average vocals.

A new musician joins us and he is also impressive on his instrument, the bass guitar. "Junior" is several years younger than me, but I'm drawn to him. He's really cute and very attentive. After a whirlwind romance, here we are in front of a justice of the peace, repeating our wedding vows.

Oh, no. What did I get myself into this time? Junior is on drugs and goes into hallucinating fits of rage. We just got home from a gig and he's throwing himself around the living room of my trailer, bouncing from one wall to the next. He's screaming and yelling at me throughout the night and early morning. Concerned for my safety, several of the band members coaxed me out to stay somewhere safe. They confront him the next day and finally he leaves the band and me. Moving back into the trailer, the locks on the doors changed, I begin to feel safe enough to stay there alone. He's gone, out of my life—but we're still legally married. Not knowing where he is, I just stay married because I can't afford a divorce anyway.

During this time, another female singer is performing in nightclubs around the area at the same time we are. Diane Cannavo is very classy. She has the qualities of a movie star. She's tall, at least 5'8", and glides across the room with elegance and grace…like how I would describe Grace Kelly or Audrey Hepburn. She embraces her audience with warmth and charm. Her hair is dark brown, and her eyes match her hair color. Her Italian ancestry lends to her beauty…Sophia Loren comes to mind. When she smiles at you, it's as if you're the only person in the room. Her voice is as smooth as silk, like Doris Day or Judy Garland. I want to be her.

I'm not even close. At 5'1", I compare myself to Betty Boop and I want to sing like Barbra Streisand. Diane and I don't know each other, but we know of each other. I don't feel worthy enough to even tie her shoe, but I wish we were friends. Little did I know that she would become a very significant influence in my life.

Being in the nightclub scene is very hard on me. Working nights and weekends makes it very difficult to visit with my children. Quitting the band, I decide to go back to work at the restaurant I worked at when I was a teenager—the same place I met Kirk and my first husband.

In walks this tall, handsome man, and sure enough, I get to wait on him. Dan is from Ohio, here on business. He's one of the nicest guys I've ever met. He doesn't hit on me like most of the guys who come in here do. He's got work in town for two weeks, and every night he sits in my station or at the bar, and we talk. *He's leaving in a matter of days. I shouldn't be thinking about him SO much. This is not smart.*

5

Help, God!
I Can't Afford a Psychiatrist!

After two weeks, Dan leaves to go back to Ohio. Two months later, much to my complete surprise, Dan walks into the restaurant. I drop everything and escort him to my station. He is here on another business trip for the next two weeks.

While he was here, we became very close. He came in every night for dinner. After my shift, we would sit at the bar and talk. This night we closed down the restaurant. Not wanting to end the night, I went to his hotel room.

"Oh my God, what time is it?"

Dan stirs next to me. "It's almost six," he says, looking at the clock on the nightstand. I'm still dressed, with a blanket gently covering me. Immediately I jump up, kiss him lightly on the cheek and head for home.

Two weeks' time flies by. Dan is headed back to Ohio. We talk on the phone every night and he arranges to come up to visit during his vacation. I wish it wasn't a long-distance relationship, but I'm enjoying him very much and look forward to talking with him when he calls. Maybe there's a plus side to having to take things more slowly—we're getting to know each other and we're developing intimacy without sex, which is a new and powerful experience for me.

> Maybe there's a plus side to having to take things more slowly—we're getting to know each other and we're developing intimacy without sex, which is a new and powerful experience for me.

At the end of the summer in 1979, he comes up to New York for a visit. Talks begin about me moving to Ohio. *Something in me just knew it.* Several weeks later, Dan flies into Albany Airport. With all my earthly belongings stuffed into a green plastic garbage bag, we jump into my Silver Buick Apollo and head to Ohio.

Immediately I apply for a job at Montgomery Inn, a local restaurant in Cincinnati. Fortunately, they're hiring and I start work tomorrow! The apartment situation is not great. This place I found in the newspaper "want ads" is run down, not especially clean and there are bugs. Bugs and I do NOT get along. Whining and complaining, I finally persuade Dan to let me move in with him. Thank God. Living alone in that place was lonely and creepy. At least I feel safe and taken care of living with Dan. After moving in with him, we finally consummate our relationship. He makes me feel complete and I love him.

Dan is a workaholic. Working on projects takes him away for 24 to 36 hours at a time. His family is a joy to be with. I love the time with his dad, Poppa Bob, Momma B and his sister, Valerie. We spend every Sunday together playing games, reading, and taking long naps.

My newfound happiness is tainted with deep sadness. Missing my kids, my family and friends in New York is a constant ache in my heart. Being alone here in Dan's small apartment is very difficult. Party girl that I am, life here is pretty boring. Dan doesn't dance nor does he care for the nightclub scene.

Donna, what are you doing? You're living with Dan. You're still married to Junior. You're living in sin. Bad girl, bad girl. After working a lunch shift, I walk into an empty house. Spending a lot of time alone is frustrating. These thoughts won't let up. Guilt, shame…could I possibly just make friends with depression, grief, and loneliness? *I'm a mess.*

Visiting several churches in the area, I keep trying to find a pastor who will help me. And by that, I mean sympathize with my choices and make me feel better about them. Not one pastor will tell me it's okay to live with Dan. "You're committing adultery and you're causing him to sin also." Well, this isn't working. No one will condone my sin. Well, the priest in New York did.

Cincinnati has several Christian bookstores. This book, *The Late Great Planet Earth*, by Hal Lindsey, looks interesting. When I walk in the door at home, it's quiet. Dan's still at work. Of course. Plopping down into the middle of the couch, I open the book and begin to read. *Holy crap! This is unreal.* The essence of the book is that Jesus Christ is coming for His perfect church, only those who believe in Him and have confessed their sin. One day, without warning, Jesus Christ will appear in the clouds. All His people, the living and the dead, will be transported to heaven right before some really devastating events happen here on earth. Those who don't believe in Jesus Christ, or are living in sin, will be left behind to go through all the predicted devastation noted in the book: Fires, wars, plagues, famines, and murder, for example.

Everyone will be forced to take a mark on their forehead or in their hand in order to buy or sell anything. This is called the mark of the beast. If you refuse, and especially if you decide to follow Jesus after the "rapture," you will be subject to torture and a violent death. *This is terrifying!!!!* I want to get out of here before all this happens. I don't want to be left behind. This book is terrifying. All I can see is this big guillotine ready to chop off my head. Fortunately, there seems to be a way out. I just have to find it.

Oh my gosh, I'm doubled over in pain. This period is debilitating. Bleeding heavily and in excruciating pain, I decide to see a gynecologist. We decide that I need a total hysterectomy. Dan and I worked together to set up our bedroom for aftercare. He bought a TV and the room was decorated for my comfort.

Before the surgery, I plan a trip to go to New York to see my kids and family. Convinced I won't make it through the surgery, I want to see everyone before my demise on the operating table.

The Point of No Return

My flight just landed at Albany International Airport. *Ah, my feet are on New York soil once again. I love New York.* As I approach the escalator to go down to Baggage Claims, I see the beautiful smiles of my siblings, Pat, Debby, Cindi, Lisa, Lori, Judy, Gregg and

Mom. Waving excitedly, I gaze on their precious, smiling faces, and happiness overwhelms me. My mother slowly walks over to me, puts my face in her hands, looks in my eyes and I see her tears welling up. "Oh, how I've missed you, Donna. I'm so glad you're home and you're safe." *What's gotten into her?*

"I missed you too, Mom." Not feeling the same sentiment towards her, I turn and rush over to the baggage carousel to get my suitcase which hasn't arrived yet. We all embrace and the busy chatter begins in the Baggage Claims area. Oh, how I've missed my family. We all pile into my mother's car, chattering all the way to her house. My mom's house will be my place of residence for about ten days. *Thankfully, I won't have to pay her rent.*

Tricia, Donald, and Tami. Look at you beautiful kids. How you've grown in just a few short months. All three of them run to greet me. As they wrap their arms around me, all at the same time, all I can feel is numb. There's this veil or cloud around my eyes and I can't see through it. My feelings of love, where are they? *What's wrong with me? You haven't seen your kids in five months? Where's the love?*

It's an hour and a half drive back to my mom's place. Pain seizes my heart. My mind is riddled with confusion, fuzziness, and numbness. *What is wrong with me?* These thoughts keep running over and over in my head and won't stop. *What's wrong with you Donna? You're in sin living with Dan, you're rotten to the core. You have no love in your heart for your own kids?? How can a mother not feel love for her children?*

Pulling into Mom's driveway, I have no idea how I made it back to her house after a long drive. An hour and a half up there and another hour and a half back is exhausting.

Feeling like an egg about to crack into a million pieces, I'm relieved that no one is near as I sneak back into my room. This is the same room Mom and Daddy slept in before he died. Shutting the door behind me and pushing the lock for privacy, I let floodgates open and burst through the dam built up around my heart. Sobbing uncontrollably, I cried out to Jesus Christ and asked Him to forgive me for all my sins. *Help God! I can't afford a psychiatrist! I feel like I'm going crazy. I need you more than ever. What kind of mother am I? I love my children, why can't I feel it?*

"Jesus, I promise I will not sleep with another man outside of marriage. If I'm supposed to stay married to Junior, let it be. If not, get me out of it. My life is totally and completely committed to you, Jesus. I don't want religion, I want a true, honest relationship with you."

Pulling myself together, I go into the bathroom, wash my face, and make a call to Pastor Sam. He couldn't come but his assistant came to the house. We sit on the stairs leading to the basement and he says, "Donna, you're living in sin with Dan and you're causing him to live in sin. You're still married and you're committing adultery. You really need to get things straightened out here. I suggest you call Dan and tell him you can't go back." Knowing he's right, but trembling inside from head to toe, he stays with me as I decide I need to make this extremely, excruciating phone call.

With every bit of strength left in me, I pick up the phone. "Dan, this is hardest thing for me to say. I cannot come back."

I can hear the shock and upset in his voice. "We can work this out. Come back, have the surgery, and we'll figure things out." It's hard to hear how hurt and desperate he sounds. I don't like causing him grief, not one bit, but my resolve has taken over my heart.

"I can't. There are so many things I have to work through here. I'm an absolute mess emotionally, physically, and spiritually. I need time and space to work through all these issues. Please forgive me. My intent is not to hurt you but to commit my life to Jesus Christ. This is more important to me than anything. I've made a mess out of my life for years. It's time to figure out how to live as a Christian."

A new strength and peace wash over me. The wall I built around my heart to keep the hurt away regarding my kids is lifting. Unfortunately, I can feel another wall building and that's towards Dan. In order to keep my commitment to Jesus, I put up a block in my heart. This is the only way I can see to help keep my commitment to Jesus and stay in New York. Otherwise, I'll hop on the first plane back to Cincinnati. My desire to follow Jesus Christ is my first and foremost priority.

Arrangements are being made with a young man who goes to my family's church. He is going on a mission trip to Tennessee. Taking my airline ticket, we changed it so he could fly into Cincinnati airport.

Dan met John at the airport with all my clothes, books and music. Within a week, it's official, New York is now, once again, my home.

Let the Lessons Begin

Now what? My surgery in Ohio is cancelled. Fortunately, I have health insurance through the job I had at Montgomery Inn. My new doctor in New York schedules some tests. After seeing the results, I'm scheduled for a total hysterectomy. My insides are a disaster. He said he couldn't see the ovaries and there was a cyst the size of a baseball attached to the pelvic wall. Adhesions from previous surgeries wrapped around my intestines, ovaries, and bowels. "You cannot go to work, do any heavy lifting or strenuous activity. This is very serious." My fear of dying on the operating table could become a reality.

Okay, God. How am I going to manage without a job? I have car insurance and a car payment. How am I going to take care of myself right now?

Lesson #1

Standing in the kitchen, thinking about what to do for lunch, I hear the Lord's quiet voice—not a whisper, just a soft, flawless, very faint voice that seems to land not on my ears but on my heart. "Donna, give your sister Lori two dollars for gas."

That's a lot of money for me right now, God. I only have ten bucks in my checking account. That's all the money I have to my name. My car payment is due, and the car insurance, and I need to get a New York driver's license.

"Give your sister two dollars for gas."

I look up to the ceiling and shake my checkbook heavenward. "Okay, God, but you're gonna have to take care of me." This was me putting God to the test to see if he would take care of me like a dad when I listened to his instruction. *Remember when your dad told you not to marry too young and you didn't listen. Okay, I get the point.* Lori got $2.00 for gas.

Several days later when the mail comes, Mom hands me a letter. It's a card from Aunt Nancy. What?! There's a check for $100.00. My relatives had taken up a collection for me. Shortly after, I receive a notice from my insurance. Dan paid my car insurance. My call to the bank went better than I could have hoped—they put a hold on my car payments until I am able to return to work.

Another important-looking piece of mail arrives the same week. It's a summons. Junior is suing me for divorce. This is great news! Everything I asked God for, he has taken care of! Here it is about a week after committing my life to Christ, and He's taken care of all my needs. All worry and fear about the surgery is slowly dissipating. Trust is building in my heart for my God, my Father, my precious Savior.

As I'm being wheeled into the operating room, I feel peace replacing fear. A new trust. *Thank you, Father, for taking care of me through this surgery. If I die, I will be with you and that will be the ultimate healing.*

Waking Up

I start to open my heavy eyes, feeling groggy…and I remember where I am. I see the bare mint-green walls of my hospital room— I've just had my surgery. Suddenly, I remember the first surgery I had when my daddy came in as I was waking up. I imagine he's here, looking at me, smiling. While it's nice to picture him here, the thought of him is not accompanied by the hard grip of grief. I don't feel the intense longing for his comfort, guidance, and love—all the crucial things I lost and have been desperately chasing after ever since he died. No, even as his image fades and leaves me with only an awareness of a dull pain in my abdomen, I simply have pleasant thoughts of him. This is very different than missing him because I felt unsafe and unloved. That need, in fact, has been filled by a different Father, and the sudden, sharp clarity of this literally makes me catch my breath.

Thanking God for everything, it occurs to me I have found my daddy—my Heavenly Father—a perfect Father who loves me, comforts me, cares for me and provides for me. He is everything I need. He's the only One I want to worship, the only One I want to be like. Other singers, actresses, other people I admire—none of them measure up to my Heavenly Father.

Thanking God for everything, it occurs to me I have found my daddy—my Heavenly Father—a perfect Father who loves me, comforts me, cares for me and provides for me.

My heart is washed anew. I am forgiven for every transgression, every mistake, everything I've ever done. Because of Jesus Christ and His sacrifice on the cross, I can stand before Him without guilt and shame. Nothing I can do will ever take the place of what Jesus did for me. I am changed in an irreversible way.

This life as a follower of Christ is going to be quite the big adventure. There's so much more I need and want to learn! So many questions I need answered. For the first time in my life, I feel confident that my tomorrows will be bright. This is the first day of the rest of my life, and I'm finally awake to enjoy it, with much gratitude to God, my Heavenly Father and my precious Jesus.

Part II

Life After Christ…
Is Really Hard

Help, God!

Part II

INTRODUCTION

"Have I not commanded you? Be strong and courageous. Do not be afraid; do not be discouraged, for the LORD your GOD will be with you wherever you go" (Joshua 1:9).

My greatest and deepest desire for you is to see you connect, or reconnect, with your Heavenly Father. To see how loving, compassionate, and empathetic He is when you're at your wits end because of the hardships and struggles that are all consuming. As He did for me in my search for a man like my dad, He revealed Himself to me and became my forever hero. He wants to be your hero too. To see you walk in the joy of knowing Him, loving Him and accepting His love for you would be my greatest reward and worth all the effort put into writing my memoir.

My deepest desire in writing "Part Two: Life After Christ is Really Hard," is to help those of you who have been confused or even hurt in a religion they grew up in or are a part of currently. Some of you have been devastated because of what is often termed "church hurt" and have no desire to go back to church or even to God. My message is not about church or religion. It's about building a relationship with a living, breathing, caring, unseen Father who desires to break you out of some of the heavy, erroneous teachings of religion, so He can wrap you in His tender loving arms to heal your wounds and hurts. This happened for me and I know it can happen for you, too.

Matthew 11:28-30 says, "Come to me, all you who are weary and burdened and I will give you rest. Take my yoke upon you and learn from me, for I am gentle and humble in heart, and you will find rest for your souls. For my yoke is easy and my burden is light."

As I share my church experiences, be assured I am not bashing any religion or church. My heart's desire is to share things I learned in several Christian churches that I personally have been a part of and how they affected my life. While trying to sift through "religion" I had to look to my Counselor, the Holy Spirit, for guidance and help to unravel through the seemingly insurmountable pile of confusion that permeated my thoughts day and night. At the same time, a multitude of pain and hurts from my life before Christ also had to be healed. Old thoughts of being stupid, grief of losing my dad and my children, hating my mother, guilt and shame. Through every situation, as I cried out to God for help, He showed me what to do and how to apply what He was trying to teach me. I learned that following His guidance was the best course to take instead of relying on my own selfish desires. Every question I asked was answered through the Bible. I had many a surprise. The cool thing is, He continues to surprise me with new things every day.

For you, as you seek God the Father, first through Jesus Christ, you will see that He has your best interest at heart. He will place His precious Holy Spirit within you. When you surrender to Him, He will lovingly, with compassion and empathy, guide you along the path. Proverbs 3:5-6 tells us, "Trust in the Lord with all your heart and lean not on your own understanding. In all your ways acknowledge Him and He will make your paths straight."

As you do your own research, and work to reconnect with your Heavenly Father, you can expect these rewards:

1. Peace as you surrender

2. Understanding that the Christian life is hard but you can get through tough stuff when the Holy Spirit fills you with courage and strength to keep moving towards Him, not away from Him.

3. Excitement when the Holy Spirit shows answers to your prayers through your research, especially in the Word.

4. Joy will permeate your heart, even in the midst of trials and difficult times (James 1:1-18).

There are so many more rewards He has in store for you. Ahead in Part II, I share some of the ways the Holy Spirit worked with me to find answers, to fall in love with God, and how to forgive myself and others.

You are so loved and are on your way to great Blessings.

Help, God!

6

Religion vs. The Holy Spirit

First Church Experience

My sister Pat and I walk into Catholic mass alone for the first time. Pat is six and I am seven. At one point during the service, we see a number of people getting up and walking to the front of the church. "Pat, do you want to go up there?" I whisper.

"Sure," she says and we both scoot to the center aisle and follow the slow-moving line of tall people in front of us. Not quite sure where we are going or what we are supposed to do, we follow the adults. I see people kneeling on padded benches that stretch across the front of the altar. On the other side of the benches is a solid marble and gold railing. I guess it's there to keep us from walking up onto the altar. It's our turn to go forward to kneel on the bench.

I see a priest on the other side of the railing. I watch him as he stands in front of one person then moves to the next one, then the next one. I see people kneeling on the bench next to me with their hands folded and heads bowed. When the priest stands in front of them, they lift their heads up, open their mouths and take what looks like a small piece of bread. Following their example with my hands folded, I lift my head, open my mouth and the priest places a piece of bread on my tongue. I'm thinking *this tastes like cardboard, what is it?* It's very dry and gets stuck to the roof of my mouth. After taking the bread, I keep my hands folded and bow my head. Pat does the same and we continue to kneel. I'm content here, and not bored like usual. Finally, we walk back to our seats.

We sit through the rest of mass and as people start leaving, I see a lady walking towards us. She's wearing a bright green dress and white gloves with a ruffle around the wrist. She has a white mantilla placed as a covering on her head. She comes over to us and I'm guessing she wants to say hello. She smiles, looks down at us and asks, "Have you two made your first Holy Communion?" I think to myself, *Um, what is that?*

I turn to Pat and give her a quizzical look. I am too afraid to ask what the lady means so I tell her, "Yes."

"Well, I don't think you realize it, but you both took the Communion twice. You're only supposed to take it once." Pat and I just look at each other as we flushed with embarrassment. We shrug our shoulders, turn around, and walk out the door without saying goodbye. We walk as fast as we can to get home so we don't have to see that "nice" lady again.

A couple of years later, I realize what that nice lady was talking about when I finally made my first Holy Communion during a special ceremony. I am dressed in all white—my dress, gloves, white patent leather shoes and socks, and a beautiful white veil.

I feel something I can't say I've ever felt before; it's pure and sweet. I love the feeling of inner peace I have as I walk to the church with my family.

After an explanation from the priest about what Communion is, I feel a sense of awe. The priest said he has the power to change the piece of bread into the actual body and blood of Jesus Christ. The Son of God's body is alive in the bread and when I take the bread He lives in my heart.

I guess Jesus leaves my heart when I commit a sin like telling a lie, disobeying my mother, or missing mass on Sunday. Every Saturday I have to go confess my sins to the priest, then he tells me what my penance is. It might be ten Our Father or five Hail Mary prayers. If the sin is really bad, like lust or anger, then I might have to pray the whole rosary. After I do this then I can go to Communion on Sunday. Let's just say I had to pray the rosary a LOT.

Communion becomes very important to me, even as a 10-year-old. I picture in my mind a tiny Jesus nailed to the cross alive in the cardboard tasting piece of bread. After I take it, it sticks to the roof of my mouth. Now I picture Jesus being torn to shreds as I begin to pick at it with my fingers. *Jesus, I'm so sorry, I don't want to hurt you but I can't get this unstuck. Please forgive me for hurting you,* is all that goes through my young and innocent mind. My heart is in turmoil. I think about Jesus getting into my soul, but totally torn to bits in the process. I truly believe Jesus lives in the bread. How trusting and naive I am. I just know that I love Jesus and don't want to do anything to hurt Him.

I believe without question everything about my religion. As much as I struggle with hurting Jesus, I know I must confess my sins to the priest, complete my punishment, and take Communion on Sunday so Jesus will come into my heart again. It's a dilemma every week, but I continue with this ritual religiously so I can go to heaven.

A Tale of Two Marys

I attend a public school in the city. Every Wednesday one of our teachers escorts me with all the other Catholic students several blocks away to the Catholic school. We sit in Catechism Class to learn about our religion and a lot about Mary. The nuns and priests call her the "Mother of God." I am taught to worship her just like I worship God.

For my birthday, my Nana gives me a six-inch-tall ceramic statue of Mary. Her face is so lovely, painted ivory white. She has blue eyes and light pink cheeks. Her body is painted to look like a beautiful flowing gown. Her hands are folded in prayer and a blue painted veil covers her head and flows to the floor. I set her up on a small table in our living room, placing a small crown of flowers on her head. My grandmother hands me a round piece of crocheted lace to place underneath her and I sprinkle flower petals around the base. Unlike my own mother (named Mary), Jesus' mother Mary looks peaceful and sweet all of the time I stare at her.

I arrive home from school, set my schoolbooks down on my piano bench that is set in the foyer. I turn around, walk into the living room, and stop in my tracks. I fight back tears as I take in the shock of seeing sweet Mary's neck broken, her head hanging loosely over to one side. Her crown of flowers is on the table in a heap with the other flowers I put there. *How am I supposed to worship her when she has a broken neck?* I try, but to no avail. I can't get past that broken neck flopping to the side. How imperfect she looks now.

I am really angry and frustrated. Not knowing what to do, I think, *I'm going to take this whole thing apart.* I am heartbroken.

The following Christmas, Nana gives me another present. The gift is beautifully wrapped in festive Christmas paper and placed in a box with a big bow. I am thrilled to discover that my gift is a statue of Mary, but this time it's made of unbreakable plastic. Immediately, I set to building another altar in the same fashion as my previous one. This statue has a lightbulb that goes up inside of it. Attached to the lightbulb is a cord that plugs into the wall and lights up Mary, the beautiful, serene Mother of God. When she is plugged in, her beautiful light blue color glows, especially in the dark.

I walk in from school and find another horrifying scene. The whole bottom of Mary is melted like candle wax because I left the light on…or someone turned it on while I was at school. *Now what do I do?* I am overwhelmed with a flood of emotions, from sadness to guilt to anger. My statue is melted, stands lopsided, and stinks from the melted plastic. *I guess it's time to put my statues to rest.*

I pick up my pitiful little Mary and go into the closet to retrieve the one with the broken neck. Out in the backyard, I take a shovel out from under the porch and dig a hole. I place both statues in a box, place them in the hole, cover them over with dirt, say a short prayer, and walk away. They will probably push up daisies someday, but for now, I'm happy they are protectively buried in my backyard.

The Flying Nuns

On Saturday morning, I walk to the Dominican Convent next door to our church. These nuns where the big hats that look like Sally Field in the TV show. I am helping them and a couple of other kids my age to serve breakfast and lunch for people who are there for a "silent retreat." They eat and do everything together in complete quiet. They attend lectures given by the priest, and then have quiet times to reflect on the teaching. I guess they do this to try to get closer to God.

I'm small and I have a hard time reaching the table to serve them coffee and water. When I bend over to reach the cup placed in front of this very beautifully dressed young woman, the full, heavy pot tips with me and I spill piping hot coffee down her back.

In my head I am screaming *Oh my God!* Terrified I had burned her horribly and that I will get in serious trouble, I don't know what to do. In this room of absolute silence, she doesn't cry out. I can see she is about to come out of her chair as she flinches, twists and moans due to being scalded by hot coffee spilling down her back. I scurry back to the kitchen, embarrassed and in fear of severe punishment. Quickly, I start helping with the dishes and never utter a word about my part in the catastrophe. Coffee pots are off limits to me from now on.

It's amazing what fear can do to a kid, or even an adult, for that matter. She was afraid to speak and I was afraid to tell someone. How very sad for both of us.

90

I regain my composure after the coffee drama. The other kids and I reset the dining room for lunch, then run off to play on this very old, rickety elevator. It has a silver and gold gate that you pull across the entrance. Once it's shut, we take turns pushing buttons and watch the levels fly by us as we ride up and down between floors. It creaks and squeaks all the way up to the attic and then down again to the main floor in this very old building. *This building should really be condemned*, I think. Now we are bored with the slow, up and down rides. One of the kids pushes "stop" and we open the door onto a random floor. We step out, expecting it to look empty and abandoned. It's not.

We stand there facing an older nun who is sitting in a rocking chair. The room is small and dark with no windows. There's a small, twin bed tucked away in a corner. I am not only surprised to find her there, I am stunned by the fact she is not wearing her habit. Her dark grey hair is really thin and surprisingly short. I had no idea a nun ever, ever took off her habit. She looks up from her sewing and stares at us. She instantly scrunches her face into the meanest scowl I've ever seen. We all turn around and hop into the elevator, quickly pulling the gate closed and head down to the main floor. Our hearts racing, we all agree we're never going up there again. Her disapproving mean face reminds me too much of my own mother. *She looks mean* and *I don't ever want to see her again.*

I didn't come here to be reminded of my mother—I came to escape her. I come here every Saturday because it is a great way to get away from the chaos at home and I do have a heart to serve my church. Mother allows it, not knowing my motivation is to get a reprieve from her barrages of anger and my own sickening fear. I constantly think of different excuses to get me out of her house. Maybe I'll become a nun.

I love being Catholic. I love how close to God I feel during mass. I love to worship sweet, gentle Mary. I love going to confess my sins to the priest, even if I have to make them up to have something to say in the confessional. I cherish everything about church, even the smell of the incense as the priest swings that basket full of smoke back and forth during mass.

Unfortunately, Catholicism didn't give me any satisfaction outside of the church setting. Broken statues that don't talk, anger, abuse, and the disappointment I write about in Part One are not satisfying. Now I'm no longer an enamored child. Church isn't the safe haven I once clung to. My life is full of depression, bitterness, resentment, and grief. Over 20 years of being a Catholic are done for me. I leave to find my own way. And it's a disaster.

Independent Baptist

Several years after my dad's death, my mother and some of my other siblings stopped going to the Catholic church. Mom was very angry at the church, the priests, and God for many years after he died. She often says to me, "I'm so angry. We weren't allowed to practice birth control! I have eight children! And then my husband dies and leaves me alone to care for them all."

I can almost feel sympathy for her, but cannot relate to her pain. Her rant continues, "Donna, your dad always said to me, 'Mary, the Catholic church says it's a sin to practice birth control and I want us to be in heaven together.'" I look at her and am confused about how to respond.

She will not let me grieve in front of her. She lies on her bed with pictures of the family strewn out in front of her. She looks up at me with her usual scowl and I feel terror. As she glares at me,

I know she is just daring me to cry. I am the oldest of eight kids. I need to keep it all together; I cannot show any emotions because it will cause her and my younger siblings pain and hurt. I retreat, go into my room and sob uncontrollably into my pillow. I miss my dad so much. *Why did my dad have to die and not my mother? He was my hero. She hates me and I hate her.*

Yes, I wish her dead. She "had" to practice the rhythm method of birth control and, doggone it, one of those feisty little sperm got away and here I am, her first child she had to have so she could be with dad in heaven. *I wish she were there instead of him.*

Feeling unwanted, insignificant, and like a thorn in her side that's a constant irritant, I drift in and out of reality yearning to be loved. Fantasies running through my mind of pictures from pornographic books and movies, I play the role of the victim being rescued by the handsome prince. I date a lot of different boys but none of them measure up to my fantasy hero. *I'm broken and don't think I'll ever get fixed. I just want to die.* I don't have the courage to take my life. But I sure wish there was a way to escape this horrible pain, grief and depression. There must be something out there other than this constant suffering.

One day a Baptist preacher who was just starting a church in the area came to our house for a visit. A couple of my sisters started to attend. For the umpteenth time my sister Debbie approaches me. "Donna, you need to get saved. Have you accepted Jesus into your heart as your personal savior?" "Of course," I say, "I've known God all my life. You don't need to talk to me about getting saved or born again." Every time I'm around her, she keeps telling me I need to be "born again." She and a couple of my other sisters are like a broken record, insist I need to come to their church and be saved. Finally, I decide it's time to check out this church. I go forward during the altar call when the pastor asks those who want to be saved to come forward. I start going every Sunday and I respond to the altar call every time I'm there. The message of salvation resonates with me deeply.

Even though I was christened as a baby, this church teaches that we need to be submersed or dunked in water in order to be truly baptized. I understand that it's different to make the choice as an adult, and I get baptized of my own free will. My reason is that I want to go to heaven and don't want to miss my chance to be reunited with my dad.

> Even though I was christened as a baby, this church teaches that we need to be submersed or dunked in water in order to be truly baptized.

But no sense of fulfillment or peace envelopes me. I still want my "fun." I still need my outlets, sinful as they are. I crave the attention of men, love getting stoned on pot or other drugs, getting drunk, and continue pursuing the party lifestyle. But every Sunday I am in church to get "born again" (just to keep myself from going to hell).

In the Catholic church, I was taught if you are not Catholic, you are going to hell. Period. From the teaching I hear, it sounds like that if you are Catholic, you are going to hell. I'm so confused I don't know what to believe.

They also believe the gifts of healing, miracles, tongues (speaking in an unknown language), among several of the other gifts mentioned in the Bible, ended when the last apostle died.

In 1 Corinthians, Chapters 12-14 the Apostle Paul writes about the gifts of the Holy Spirit. According to Pastor Sam's teaching, and the belief of several of my family members, anyone who speaks in tongues is full of the devil. *Uh oh. I think I'm going to get in trouble here.*

A Holy Spirit Encounter

After committing my life to Christ, my friend Hope called me and asked me to go with her to see a new preacher at the Assembly of God Church. "Who is he?" I asked her. Benny Hinn just started out in ministry and I never heard of him. "Hope, I'll have to pray about it and get back to you," I tell her. I go to bed that night begin to pray, "Jesus, I'm going with Hope to see Benny Hinn. If you want me there, please keep me there. If you don't want me there, please get me out. Oh, and please don't let anyone speak in tongues." Because the Baptist teaching on "speaking in tongues" is so strong against it, I am terrified that someone might start speaking in a kind of gibberish. I am not sure about Pastor Sam's teaching. I want to learn the truth and I'm committed to go with Hope.

With fear and trembling, but learning to trust in God, I go with Hope and my sister Lori to see Benny Hinn at the First Assembly of God church.

Here I am sitting in a Pentecostal church…Am I committing a mortal sin? I don't how the Catholic church feels about a Pentecostal church. Am I playing with the devil according to the Baptist church? I'm pretty sure I know how they feel about it and I'm just trusting Jesus to guide me.

We are seated in a long hallway, our chairs placed at the entrance into a large room with a big stage up in the front. All I can see is a sea of color: purple, blue, pink, bright yellow, green, and white among the crowd. I see at least one hundred or more people, some standing, some already seated, yet I can't see many faces because we're peering in from the back of this hallway and off to the side. An usher comes up to us and says, "Sorry ladies, I have to move you because you are violating the fire code by blocking an entrance."

We get up and follow him to our new destination, and much to my distress, we wind up backstage behind the curtain and then are led out to a half-circle of chairs placed right on that big stage. My seat is the very first chair, right up front on the left-hand side of the stage. My heart starts pounding. This is a nightmare. I have terrible stage fright, I don't like heights, and I hate very bright lights. I'm thinking, I can look down over the edge of this stage and if I fall off my chair, I'm going to land on that hardwood floor. Benny Hinn comes out from behind the curtain and is now standing three feet away from where we are seated—there's no escape.

I don't want to make a scene, so I stay in my seat. I try to focus on Benny, who is now speaking to the crowd, whose faces I can now see. "We're here to reverence the Holy Spirit," he says to the crowd. "I want the house lights turned down, shut the doors coming into the gym, and I don't want anyone speaking in tongues." Flabbergasted, I almost fall out of my seat and off the stage. Both of my prayers are instantly answered.

Okay God, I'm trusting YOU to take care of me here. I'm not very comfortable with this situation at all but you answered my prayers…so here we go.

Benny concludes his message and walks off the stage, down a few steps to the floor below. I'm looking down at him and a crowd of people begin to come forward to have him pray for them. I'm watching as they begin falling like flies down onto the floor all around him and the ushers begin running around putting some kind of cloth over them as they lie on the floor. I am in awe. Is he pushing them down? He heads back up onto the stage.

There are at least 50 of us standing up in a horseshoe-like half circle. Praying out loud, he goes to the opposite side from where we are. He starts laying hands on each person, and they begin falling on the floor too. Oh my God, he's making his way around the half-circle. He prays for my sister, Lori. Her mouth flies open when he prays for her.

This is my first experience in a Pentecostal church, and I've never seen anything like this. I'm a nervous wreck, my insides are quivering like I drank way too much caffeine. What is going on? Panicked, I pray in a whisper, "God, what have you gotten me into here?"

> This is my first experience in a Pentecostal church, and I've never seen anything like this.

Fear and confusion fill me as Benny walks in my direction.

When he reaches me to pray, I feel my fear take a turn to defiance. I cross my arms, look him square in the eyes, and think, You ain't pushin' me down, Mister. He stretches his hand out towards my forehead but doesn't even touch me. His hand is about four inches away from my forehead. Much to my amazement, I land flat on my butt in my chair. I didn't fall on the floor, but a force

I never felt before touched me with a gentle push. I can't explain it; I don't understand what happened.

I feel this surge of "energy" or a sweet feeling of peace wash over me. The fear and anxiety are gone. Completely vanished. Needless to say, I am left with a LOT of confusion. What is it that pushed me down? Are the gifts really for today?

We leave to go home and Lori shares that her ears are healed and she can hear. I hurry up to my little room and cry out, "Help, God, I need you more than ever right now." I want truth, teach me fresh. I am still reeling from the hurt I experienced at the Baptist church. Questions begin stirring within me and a desire for truth becomes a raging thirst.

My search begins in my little room in a big house with lots of siblings, neighborhood kids and my mother. Oh boy, I don't know what to expect. And then, all hell breaks loose as I begin this journey to find truth.

Romans 10:8-9

"If you confess with your mouth, 'Jesus is Lord',
and believe in your heart that God raised Him
from the dead, you will be saved.
For it is with your heart that you believe and are justified,
and it is with your mouth that you confess and are saved.
As the Scripture says, anyone who trusts in Him
will never be put to shame."

Galatians 5:22

"But the fruit of the Spirit is love, joy, peace, patience, kindness
gentleness, goodness, faithfulness, and self-control."

7

Lessons in Trust

Six weeks after my surgery, Mom comes into my room, sits down on the bed next to me and says, "Donna, it's time for you to get a job. I'm going to charge you fifty dollars a month to stay here." My heart sinks and I feel like I am right back to when I was 16 years old. I panic, just like I did then when I had my first surgery and Mom said, "Donna, you need to get a job to help pay for your medical bills."

The sinking feeling hits the pit of my stomach. A wave of hurt, anger and resentment of her abuse crashes over me like Niagara Falls. Yet I know she's right about me getting a job. I really can't sit in this bed forever, convalescing. It's time for me to get up and get to work. Recovery is over.

I bite hard on my bottom lip to help push away the hurt and anger towards my mother and go into the living room to pick up the newspaper. With resentment in my heart, I open the "Help Wanted" section to look for a job. I say a prayer inside: "God,

I want a job that I like doing, transcription in a claims department at an insurance company, making five dollars an hour."

With a deep conviction, I begin to tithe at church and give where I believe God is leading me to give. In obeying God in this area of my life, I truly believe God will answer my prayer. I keep reading Malachi 3:8-12, that, to me, seems to promise that if I give into His storehouse, He will pour out on me a blessing. Ahead of receiving what I want, I thank God for providing for me. "God, I'm not giving to get from you, I just need you to take care of me just like you did when I gave my sister money for gas. I want to continue to trust You." I have a strong sense that He is teaching me that when He asks for something, it is so He can give back abundantly, not to take away anything. It's a trust issue, not a give, so he can take it away from me, issue. I cannot imagine the infinite generosity of how God pours out His blessings upon those of us who love and trust Him.

On a bright sunny morning in late summer, I walk into the American International Insurance Company. The interview is pretty standard and they offer me the job making $4.50 an hour typing insurance policies. I say, "No thank you, this is not what I'm looking for. I know I will be bored out of my mind just typing up policy information and I am looking for work that pays five dollars an hour." Back home again, I comb the newspaper for another opportunity.

I've been home three hours and now the phone rings. It's the same insurance company calling me. The woman on the phone says, "Donna, your resume was passed to me from our other department. Please come and interview with us. We have just what you're looking for and we can work to meet your hourly rate."

"No, thank you, but I'm really not interested." My mind is spinning trying to make up excuses, any excuse to not go back there for another interview. I am just not interested, not one bit. Exhausted, just the thought of driving there again is overwhelming when all I want to do is go back to bed and stay there.

She continues, "Donna, please come in. We've looked over your resume and we really want to talk to you. We are looking for someone to do transcription in another department." This piques my interest and I agree to drive the 20 minutes back down to the office to meet with them again.

I'm greeted by Terry, the woman who called me. She tells me I'm to meet with Mr. Edwards. She also explains that he is the brand-new manager in this department and it's his first day on the job. As I walk into his office, everything is in disarray. Movers are here bringing in boxes and moving furniture around in his beautiful, newly painted, bright and sunny office. Mr. Edwards is directing people to put things here and there and I'm looking at him thinking, *I don't think I'm going to take this job.*

"Hello," he says, and gestures for me to walk out with him. After a few steps down the hall, we go into the coffee breakroom. There are a number of tables with four chairs around each one. There is a counter with a coffee pot placed next to a sink. Across the small room is a refrigerator, which I imagine is for employees to put their lunch or leftovers in to take home. It is also a bright room, clean and inviting. As we sit down at one of the tables, he begins to ask me some questions. Then, much to my surprise, he offers me the job. I am hired to do transcription for the Adjusters in the Claims Department. To top it all off, he offers me $5.00 per hour!

"Yes, I'd love to accept this job. Thanks!" I say as I almost tip my chair over backward, trying to contain my excitement. God answered my prayer precisely, to a tee.

I walk out of the building and look up at the bright, cloudless sky. I feel elated and grateful. To think I almost missed this incredible opportunity. "Oh God, you are truly my Father who cares about me and I am really learning to trust in You. Thank You for taking care of me and answering my prayer."

As I begin my new job, I start completing all the necessary paperwork which seems like I'm writing a book, but I am filled with joy and gratitude at this blessing from God. I sit at my desk, facing away from my co-worker, Marian. I already feel like I'm going to like her. She is quite a character, with beautiful blond hair, gorgeous blue eyes that seem to sparkle, and a smile that lights up the room. She has a contagious personality and those gorgeous blue eyes are just full of mischief. We are sitting back-to-back about seven to eight feet away from each other. With my headphones on and typing on a brand new IBM Selectric Typewriter, my new career as a transcriptionist in the Claims Department begins. I LOVE my job and I LOVE the people I work with.

One final surprise is when I discover that an old friend and former neighbor works here. I am "the new girl" but I already feel so comfortable. On my break, I go outside and look up to the heavens. "God, you did it again," I say. "Thank You."

My Father, God, answered my prayer and gave me exactly what I asked Him to do. All I can say is that I am in awe with my new-found relationship with this Heavenly Father, unseen but so real.

Psalms 28:7
"And those who know your name put their trust in you,
for you, O Lord, have not forsaken those who seek you."

I'm learning about a new job but also learning about a new faith. This is an exciting but complicated journey for me. There is so much for me to learn about my Father God, his Son Jesus, and the Holy Spirit. It's stimulating, exhausting and somewhat scary at times, but I can't quit. It seems my desire for truth and understanding is insatiable. Running to my room every night after work to get into the Bible, attending Bible studies at the Baptist church, practically living in the Christian bookstore, reading books to help me understand my religious upbringing are all a part of my new life as a follower of Jesus Christ.

My First Church Hurt

I'm feeling good about my life for the first time in a long time. I love my new job and my deep-felt relationship with God. I begin to date a young man who attends the Baptist church. We dated for several months, going to Christian concerts, out to dinner and for drives down by the river where we'd just sit and talk to get to know each other.

One warm, Spring evening, we went to dinner and now we are sitting in the car out in front of my house. He turns and says, "This is very hard for me to say, Donna, but I was told to stay away from you, that you are like a leopard who will never change her spots. Also, because you just had a hysterectomy, we can't have kids together. I can't date you anymore."

I just stare at him and feel like I'm going to be sick. My throat is so tight I can't speak. I am dumbfounded. I turn and give him a look that says good-bye. Exiting the car, I walk toward my house without looking back. I feel like a zombie as I enter the front door. Once again, I feel like I got punched in the gut. The pain and hurt sends me into a tailspin. Reeling, feelings of rejection and abandonment overwhelm me. *How can anyone be that cruel?* I think to myself. *Can't he see the sincerity of my commitment to Christ? Yes, I had a hysterectomy and can't have kids. But can we work through this issue by adopting and building a relationship with my own children?*

What's worse is that someone in my church said that about me. I find out it came from one of the leaders. I am really mad, hurt, and disgusted. Because of my new relationship with Jesus, I know I must forgive and move on. In some ways, I am thankful for this hurt because I am now on a very intentional quest for answers about living for Jesus. I am much more aware that the only connection

> In some ways, I am thankful for this hurt because I am now on a very intentional quest for answers about living for Jesus...I don't want half-truths anymore.

that really matters is the one with God. I don't want half-truths anymore. I'm confused about Catholicism, Independent Baptists, and Pentecostals. I don't want to read the Bible to see if I am right about what I believe. I want to read the Bible to see where the Bible is right and areas in my life I need to change.

My little bedroom is now my sanctuary. After work, I hurry to get there where I feel comfortable, even though it's only the size of a walk-in closet. But it's my own space and I love it. There is a window that brightens it up and allows the moon to shine in at night. I have a twin bed with a nightstand next to it. At the end of the bed on the floor, I have my small boom box that I use to record music I hear on the one and only Christian radio station that's available in our area. Wherever I go, either for a walk or in my car, I take my boom box with a cassette tape. As soon as I hear a song come on the radio that touches my heart, I hit the Record button being careful not to record over songs I previously recorded. I'm building a repertoire of inspirational worship music that draws me closer to Jesus.

I don't feel like I need a church right now. I begin to worship, pray, and ask God questions to learn all that He wants to teach me. The things I'm discovering through the Bible are absolutely blowing my mind. *WOW, who knew?* Things that I learned all through my religious life are being revealed for what they really are: Some true, many false. I can't wait to dig in deeper and learn more about Jesus. How do I get close to Him? This journey is so exciting and rewarding and one I can't wait to share with whoever will listen.

Help, God!

8

Love God, Love Oneself

After work, I go into my room, shut the accordion sliding door, and sit down with my back against the head of my bed and my Bible on my lap. I pray out loud, "God, I ask you to wipe away everything I learned in the Catholic church, the Baptist church, and the Pentecostal church. Teach me truth from your Word. I want to know YOU more. I'm ready to dig in and to start with a clean slate."

I turn on the cassette tape player and play the song that I recorded in my car on the way home from work. As I am singing the worship song to the Lord from my heart, I ask, *God, who do I pray to? Do I pray to Mary? Joseph? Luke?* I open my brand-new King James Bible. As I begin to read, I come upon this verse in 1 Timothy 2:5-6: "For there is one God, and one mediator between God and men, the man Christ Jesus; who gave himself a ransom for all, to be testified in due time." Okay, then that settles it. No more praying to the saints for me—it's Jesus all the way.

I randomly open to another page, Exodus 20, and what I see here shocks me. I cannot believe what I am reading. I've never seen or heard this before in any of my Catholic upbringing. Exodus 20:3-5: "Thou shalt have no other gods before me. Thou shalt not make unto thee any graven image, or any likeness of anything that is in heaven above, or that is in the earth beneath, or that is in the water under the earth. Thou shalt not bow down thyself to them, nor serve them: for I the Lord thy God am a jealous God..." I close the Bible quickly and just about fall out of my bed. This is not what I learned in catechism class. I worshipped statues of Mary. I prayed to statues of the saints and baby Jesus, Jesus on the cross—they were all over the church I went to as a kid. As I begin to pray, I ask God to forgive me for bowing down to any of these statues and idols. I decide to never have any of them in my home again.

I cannot believe that I was never taught this part of the Bible before. My heart is aching but thankful for the truth of this Scripture. What more false beliefs am I going to discover?

> What more false beliefs am I going to discover?

Lord, Teach Me to Love You

I am eager to run into my private space as soon as I get home from work each day. I close the door and begin to worship and pray quietly: "Lord, teach me to love You. I am worshipping and reading my Bible, but I don't feel a lick of love in my heart for You. I want to FEEL love for You. God help me to feel it."

My worship time always includes listening to the uplifting songs I've managed to record from the radio. I only have a few, but I play them again and again on my boom box. They help me to feel love for Jesus. The more I pray, listen, and worship, the more I begin to FEEL the love rising in my heart. It is so overwhelming sometimes, I just cry because I can actually feel this love for my unseen Father, my God, my Jesus. "Thank You Lord for helping me. I want to love You deeper...help me."

I can't explain how simply taking time to worship serves to deepen my heart-felt feelings and relationship with God, but it does. I know He is with me and is answering my prayers because things actually change.

The worship songs I gravitate to are the ones that express a deep love for God, not about God—ones that tell Him how wonderful, awesome, beautiful, and great He is. They feel deeply intimate to me, are slower in tempo, and touch my heart and soul in a way that I can't describe. I just know that I am in the presence of my unseen Heavenly Father and that I can FEEL His presence. As I truly wanted, now I can feel an overwhelming love in my heart for Him. These powerful songs are not easy to find, but I keep searching and hope to add to my collection.

Lord, Teach Me to Feel How Much You Love Me

Another evening after work I am back in my sanctuary. As I'm worshipping, I begin to quietly pray, God, You answered my prayer and I can FEEL love in my heart for You. Please help me learn how much You love me.

I don't feel loved by anyone, really. I feel lonely, rejected, fearful, and in so many ways desperate. No one understands what I am going through right now. My hero Daddy is gone, I am separated from my children, Dan is in another state. The guy I was dating in the Baptist church decides to quit seeing me. I guess he thinks I'm a leopard whose spots won't change or maybe I'm contagious, like a leper. *Hmm, I'm not quite sure.*

The teachings at the Baptist church are not always comforting. I am excited to learn about God, but it is hard because I am not buying everything I'm learning here. My family doesn't understand what I'm going through. My mother seemed to be more in tune with me when I was a sinner running around with so many different men, drinking and partying all night. Now, I am really searching for more of God yet feeling more and more alone in the process. I'm learning that relationships other than the one with God are not reliable, probably because I feel like a salmon swimming upstream, going against the flow. I'm questioning everything I'm hearing right now. I want to hear from God through His Word, not from what a man thinks His Word means. I want truth, nothing but the truth, so help me God.

"God, I just really need to know that You love me," I pray. "You're the only love that matters to me right now, and I need You more than ever!"

Everyone knows John 3:16, I think, or at least has heard of it: "For God so loved the world that He gave His one and only Son, that whoever believes in Him shall not perish but have everlasting life." I begin to make this personal. I'm not sure if I heard this in a sermon, or the Lord just told me to do it, I don't know—but I took that verse and said: "If I was the only person on this earth, You would have died on that cross for me, because God so loved *me*, that He gave His one and only Son for *me*, that if I believe in Him, I will not perish but have everlasting life."

This becomes my personal affirmation. The more I recite John 3:16 this way, the stronger I feel that God loves ME and I am beginning to be CONFIDENT of the love He has for me. The best part of John 3 is found in verses 17-18: "For God did not send His Son into the world to condemn the world, but to save the world through Him. Whoever believes in Him is not condemned, but whoever does not believe stands condemned already because he has not believed in the name of God's one and only Son."

I was a part of the world and He died for me. He didn't condemn me to hell when I overdosed in Florida. He saw fit to help me when I cried out from the pit, "Jesus, don't let me die here. Help, God, this torment is awful!" Oh, I am so thankful for His love for me. *Amazing grace…that saved a wretch like me…*

I think about every word in this Scripture. What is "the world" according to the Bible? The "world" represents sinful humanity—those who live apart from God and live according to their own hedonistic desires. I know first-hand what it's like to live in "the world" and what it feels like to be saved from it.

"There is no pit so deep, that God's love is not deeper still."

—Corrie Ten Boom

A New Church Experience

As I shared previously, the Baptist church I attend teaches that the spiritual gifts died out with the last apostle. I never remember the preacher telling us who he thought that was. They believe "speaking in tongues" was a one-time event that happened on the Day of Pentecost. For them, tongues seems to be the biggest offender of all the gifts. Their "go-to" Scripture is in 1 Corinthians 13:8 that says where there are tongues, they will cease. We're taught that anyone who speaks in tongues is full of the devil and this is drilled into us continually.

In 1 Corinthians 13:8-10, we read: "Love never fails. But where there are prophecies, they will cease; where there are tongues, they will be stilled; where there is knowledge, it will pass away. For we know in part and we prophesy in part, but when perfection comes, the imperfect disappears." In this church, the belief is that the Bible is "that which is perfect." As I read this, I think, it also says prophecies will cease and knowledge will pass away. In my questioning mind, I think, *are we all walking around stupid?* Revelation 19:10 states: "For the testimony of Jesus Christ is the spirit of prophecy." Aren't we testifying about Jesus Christ and the need to be born again? *Boy, do I have a LOT to learn.* I am questioning everything and I want truth.

> I am questioning everything and I want truth.

Well, I start to regularly visit the First Assembly of God church in Schenectady, New York. Most of the teaching is about walking in faith. In all of my uncertainty, I get even more confused going here. But I am on a quest for truth. To my surprise, I see a woman who is very familiar. Oh my—Diane. I met her several years ago when I was out for my anniversary with my first husband. She carried herself with such dignity and grace. During a break from her singing on stage, she came over to our table and placed a rose on it to wish us a happy anniversary. I always thought, if I ever get to sing out like that, I want to be like her. After my divorce, when I started singing in various clubs around the area, she was also singing in local clubs. People would go see Diane and then come to see our band.

I find out that she is now born again and attends this church. I am very shy and won't introduce myself to her because I just don't feel worthy enough. I watch her from a distance. What I notice about her is that she is elegant, graceful, and contemplative. She radiates God's love and has a smile that is so beautiful it's contagious. In my heart, I just know this woman loves Jesus and I bet she speaks in tongues. She's in a Pentecostal church…she must.

Since my encounter with Benny Hinn, I have been thinking about the gifts, especially the gift of tongues. One of the things I remember about my teaching in the Baptist church is a song from this Scripture: Galatians 5:22: "But the fruit of the spirit is love, joy, peace, patience, kindness, goodness, faithfulness, gentleness and self-control. Against such

> Galatians 5:22: "But the fruit of the spirit is love, joy, peace, patience, kindness, goodness, faithfulness, gentleness and self-control. Against such things there is no law."

things there is no law." I begin to think that the opposite of the *fruit of the spirit* is the *fruit of the devil*. What would be the fruit of the devil? *Hmm…The opposite of love is hate, the opposite of joy is sadness, the opposite of peace would be turmoil/chaos…* A picture of Diane comes to mind and I don't see anything that looks like the fruit of the devil. The fruit of the spirit is very evident in her demeanor when I see her at church. I have not seen anything in this church that resembles the fruit of the devil. Everything is done decently and in order. I feel like I am learning better discernment on my journey to search for truth.

Pastor Larson is the first pastor I meet here. He has taken me under his wing and is teaching me so much. I begin to call him Papa Larson, as he is full of wisdom and reminds me of own dad. He's compassionate and caring. The love of Christ exudes from him and his wife as they help me through some of the things I am dealing with, such as my confusion about the gifts of the spirit and how they are working in my life. I'm so thankful because I was beginning to think I was crazy. Some things I began to discern at an early age, such as knowing I couldn't tell my mom about that dirty old man, or the dream about my dad before he died. God was moving in my life even then and I didn't realize it. Now, my confidence is beginning to grow. I don't feel like I'm full of the devil, or that I'm a leopard or leper. How refreshing to be with others who understand what I'm going through, and who desire to help me grow in Jesus.

Back in my bedroom, I begin searching for Scriptures about the Holy Spirit and speaking in tongues. I can practically recite by heart what I am being taught at the Baptist church. It is so sad how vehemently opposed it is to the gifts of the Spirit, particularly tongues. Beginning to read Acts 19, my mouth flies open in awe and my whole world is turned upside down.

I close my eyes and, in my mind, I go back over what I had just read. So, the Apostle Paul was walking on a road and arrived in Ephesus. There he found some men and asked them if they had received the Holy Spirit when they believed. They said that they hadn't even heard of the Holy Spirit. So, Paul placed his hands on them, the Holy Spirit came on them, and they spoke in tongues and prophesied. There were about 12 men in all. All of a sudden, my eyes fly open and I have clear understanding: Paul wasn't there on the Day of Pentecost when they were all speaking in tongues after they received the Holy Spirit. Paul wasn't even a Christian at the time. He prayed for these men in Ephesus and they received the Holy Spirit. WOW...the gifts ARE for today.

As I look up, I excitedly raise my hands to the Lord in heaven. I wish I could shout out at the top of my lungs, but I hold back, fearing someone in the house might hear me. I shout in a loud whisper, "I believe, Lord! The gifts are for today, and I want them, every one of them!"

"I believe, Lord! The gifts are for today, and I want them, every one of them!"

I turn off my light, lie down in bed, and begin to pray. All of a sudden, I feel and actually see three snickering demonic spirits laughing in the corner of my bedroom window. I can hardly breathe and my heart feels like it's going to beat right out of my chest, I am so scared. "He that is in me is greater than he that is in the world!" I say over and over. I'm not quite sure exactly what that means but it's the only Scripture I can think of right now. Then without warning, I hear POP, POP, POP...and those faces are gone.

My room suddenly fills with this very light feeling, like something dark and heavy was pushed out and away. I get up onto my knees and open my mouth to pray. I hear my voice, but don't comprehend the words.

What language is this? I'm speaking in an unknown tongue. It sounds something like French, which is funny because part of my ancestry is French. I feel as light as a feather, and I am immersed in this sweet, light presence that encompasses my whole body. Is this what it feels like to be born again? It's as though I'm in the cocoon of light that overtakes me, even any and all darkness in my soul.

All of a sudden, I hear my sister Lori running out of her bedroom which is just down the hall from mine. She starts yelling, "Who's down there, who's jumping up and down?!" No one else is inside. Without turning on the light in my bedroom, I open the door and walk out into the hallway. My sister looks at me and says, "Donna, are you alright? You look like you saw a ghost."

I say, "I did, the Holy Ghost. There was a battle for my soul between Jesus and the devil and Jesus WON." We hear the family coming into the house. I look down from the top of the stairs to see Lori running down to tell everyone what happened. This experience is meant to be between me and God, but all of a sudden it becomes very public. Oh, no. I'm sure all hell's about to break loose.

My mom screams at me, "I don't want you chanting in your room!" Some of my other sisters are now convinced I am full of the devil. What a dilemma. My beautiful experience is shrouded in anger and upset. I am very much alone in my deep-felt joy. It is so beautiful, and I vow to never let it go. I know it is God the Holy Spirit and I know His love has permeated my whole being.

Now it's the next day, and I go see Pastor Sam of the Baptist church. "Pastor Sam, I had this experience in my room." He's sitting at his dining room table. When I tell him, his face turns bright red. With his head down, both hands clenched into fists, he explodes in anger. Pounding on the dining room table, he speaks in a loud, commanding voice, "You go home and forget about this! It was just an emotional experience. Forget it ever happened."

Stunned for a moment, I take a breath and say, "Pastor Sam, I cannot forget this. It was real and Jesus touched me in a powerful way that I will never forget." In his fury, I am basically kicked out of the house. As I step out of his front door and onto the small porch, I close the door behind me. Taking a deep breath, I hear the Lord's still, small voice. Donna, he's responsible for his attitude between me and him, and you are responsible for your attitude towards me and you. Forgive him and go on. In this moment, I totally and completely forgive Pastor Sam for being so angry with me. My prayer is that one day he will see the truth about this incredible gift.

I've been visiting the First Assembly of God church in Schenectady and I'm in a quandary—do I stay at the Baptist church or go to this Pentecostal church? Papa Larson advises me to continue to visit First Assembly of God for four weeks in a row and then I will know where I'm supposed to be. At the end of four weeks, I decide it's going to be my church home.

The decision to go to the Pentecostal church brings loneliness with it. Some family members think I'm out of my mind and full of the devil. When I want to worship with my family and go to visit the Baptist church, I'm not allowed to take Communion because I am no longer a part of their church family. Several of my siblings are sitting there yet I can't partake of Communion with my family. No longer in the Catholic church and no longer a part of the Baptist church, I feel alone except for my relationship with God. I am thankful for Papa Larson and the Pentecostal church, but it's still not like family.

Some of my Catholic family members are begging me to return to the Catholic church; some of my Baptist family and friends are pretty harsh with me about the whole speaking in tongues issue. I am doing my best to respect where they are, but I am not about to relinquish my newfound freedom in Christ through the Holy Spirit. It is their responsibility if they choose to judge me and mine if I choose to judge them. I will never forget the beautiful experience I had in my small sanctuary. Galatians 5:22 continues to resonate within my heart. "The fruit of the Spirit is love, joy, peace, gentleness, goodness, faith, meekness, temperance and longsuffering." If the fruit of the Spirit continues to grow within me, and it shows on the outside, I know I'm not full of the devil.

> It is their responsibility if they choose to judge me and mine if I choose to judge them.

As a new believer filled with the Holy Spirit, my zeal and impulse to share with others can have an opposite effect of what I want. I would love for others to experience what I have. It's so good, I want to give it away to my children and to my family. It's such a beautiful, awesome thing to have this deep relationship with Jesus. They have it too, I know, but feeling one's whole heart and soul so full of love is pure joy. To try and explain it is next to impossible unless they experience it themselves.

My children and I meet and visit when I can afford to drive the hour-and-a-half to see them. I love them so much and hope they see and feel how much happier and more grounded I am now that I have Jesus filling my heart. My prayer is that they will all come to know Christ as intimately as I have been blessed to do.

9

Divine Moves of God

"Donna, you need to move out from under your mother's influence. She has an evil spirit."

I'm hearing this from a man I respect, Papa Larson, as I sit across from him in his church office. "You need to come out from under her control," he continues, "I know a young woman who is in a difficult spot and is looking for someone to rent a room in her home. Would you be interested?"

"I would love to," I respond, "but how much and where?" I hope the rent won't be more than what I am able to pay, which is what my mother is charging me ($50 a month).

I learn that Diane, the woman who sang in the nightclubs, who I have noticed at church, is looking for someone to rent a room. I could not be more surprised! Papa Larson has no idea about my "relationship" to Diane. How God put this together boggles my mind. *God, You really are taking care of me and You know exactly what*

I need. Thank you! Papa Larson and I go to her home to meet her. With the cost per month lower than what I am now paying, I know this will be a good move. Diane and I enjoy each other so much; and we have so much in common. We are both so excited and can't wait for me to move in. *Oh boy, how do I tell Mom I'm moving out.*

As I walked in the house, Mom is sitting on the sofa in the living room reading one of her favorite magazines. "Mom, I need to talk to you. I just had a meeting with an old friend who is renting a room at her house."

"Oh?" she responds lowering the magazine from under her nose.

"Yes, I've decided it's time for me to move out. She has a room for rent and I'm moving in this weekend."

"Sounds like a good idea. I can give your room to your brother. He wants to move upstairs so this will work out perfectly." *Great, I think she's relieved. And now she doesn't have to worry about me chanting in my room.*

Mom goes back to reading her magazine and I head upstairs to pack up all my worldly goods. Shouldn't be much of a job since I live in a room the size of a walk-in closet. *Wow, that went a lot better than I expected.*

Within a few days it is done and I'm out of her house.

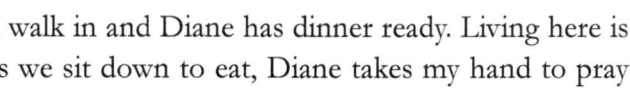

After work, I walk in and Diane has dinner ready. Living here is such a joy. As we sit down to eat, Diane takes my hand to pray over the meal. At the end of her prayer she says, "Donna, are you hearing anything from God?"

With my head bowed and my mind almost a blank, I hear nothing.

"No," I answer sheepishly.

I'm trying with all I'm worth to hear something. *I want to hear your voice, God!* In quiet whispers, sometimes when I am walking outside or eating breakfast by myself, I hear Him—but in prayer, I do not. Oh, but I so desire to hear Him more and more.

I feel like a child at times, and Diane is teaching me so much. She encourages me musically, helps me to pray, and shares the Scriptures with me. I love staying here, but most of all, I am grateful to begin feeling that I trust her and love her dearly as a friend and sister in Christ.

First Demonic Encounter

It's midnight and I am startled awake as the phone rings. It's Marian from work, and she is yelling over the phone, "He's got me! He's throwing me around and I need help, can you come?" Since we've had many conversations about her belief that the Devil literally attacks her, I tell her yes. I immediately call Papa Larson. Even at this late hour, he agrees to go with me. Driving separately, we meet up in the parking lot of her apartment building. When I pull up, I see him parked waiting for me. He motions for me to get into his car. I jump in and he says to me.

"Before we go in, we must repent of anything we've done that's displeasing to the Lord and ask Him to forgive us." We join hands, and take turns confessing to each other and ask Jesus for protection.

"Father, I ask that you forgive me for being angry with my mother this afternoon. Thank you for your forgiveness and protection as we meet with Marian."

Papa Larson prays, then we get out of the car, walk up to her front door, and press the button to her apartment. I hear the buzzer and open the door to enter the building.

We walk up the stairs and press the doorbell to Marian's apartment. She opens the door, but as we step in, she suddenly backs up against the wall, goes from rigid to slack, then slithers down it like a snake, landing flat on the carpet. I stare, my jaw dropping. Papa Larson looks at her and says, "Are you done?"

Marian opens her eyes, looks up at him, and says, "Yes," then proceeds to get up off the floor.

We walk over to sit in chairs around a glass-top table. Papa Larson starts to pray out loud. As soon as the name of Jesus Christ is mentioned, Marian again goes stiff, closes her eyes, goes slack and slithers like a snake out of her chair onto the floor.

It's impossible to comprehend what I am witnessing. All I can think of is Olive Oil, the female character in the *Popeye* cartoons I watched as a kid. Olive Oil would get into some kind of trouble, go stiff as a board, then she would conform to the shape of her chair, an ironing board, or whatever object she happened to be near at the time. I feel confused and scared as I sit here watching Marian, her eyes closed, lying on the floor.

Papa Larson stands up from his chair, looks down at her, and says, "Okay, are you done yet?"

"Yes," she replies, and then she gets up. The rest of the conversation is a blur but we pray for peace over her and leave.

I'm home, trying to quiet my mind and go to sleep. It's 2 a.m. I start to ask God for understanding but fall fast asleep.

The next day at work, with my back to her and my headphones on as we both are typing away, I am praying for her under my breath. My heart wants her to be spiritually free of any evil, but the nearly silent prayer is coming out in whispered tongues (my newfound language). Marian whips around in her chair, and with an intense glare, and in a deep, guttural growl, she says to me, "What are you doing?"

I say, "I'm praying for you."

She says, "Well, quit it." I just smile and turn my back to her and continue with my work. In all honesty, I am quite disturbed as I've never encountered this before, at least not as blatantly as her reaction. I know some dark force is afoot, but all I can think to do is pray for her, and be here for her if she calls on me.

In many ways, God used Marian to bless me. Luke 6:38 says: "Give, and it will be given unto you; good measure, pressed down, shaken together and running over shall men give into your bosom." As I'm learning to trust God by tithing and giving to others in need (like my sister who needed two dollars for gas), He, in turn, is using Marian to give me money…lots of money. I open my desk drawer to find an envelope with $50, $100, and one time $500 to fix my car that had been damaged. I try my best to give the money back and she refuses.

One Sunday morning, Marian calls and asks if she can come to church with me. "Absolutely, please come." She drives over and rides with me. When we return back to my place, she hands me an envelope with cash in it.

"I cannot accept this," I tell her.

Marian turns and looks me right in the eye and says, "Look, I am independently wealthy, and I'm trying to learn to give—and you need to learn to receive." I'm shocked. I don't know what to say.

"Thank you, I'm not looking to take your money, honestly."

Marian doesn't let up. "This is for you, now take it." Reluctantly I thank her and take the $100 gift she put in the envelope.

Later, thinking more about our encounter, I start to realize that the Devil will twist Scriptures to use for his purposes. In the book of Matthew, Chapter 4, Satan uses portions of Scripture to tempt Jesus. Acts 20:35 says, "It is more blessed to give than to receive." Marian, says, "I'm learning to give, you need to learn to receive." Being a new believer, I didn't know if what she said is actually Scripture. I give from my heart because I care. Satan twists the Scripture to control me so I will take care of Marian. She gives me money, then, out of my sense of obligation, I help her with an endless number of errands and chores..

We go into the house after our discussion in the car. We have lunch, along with Diane and another friend. When we begin to talk about Jesus, the bread in the oven catches on fire! Marian laughs as Diane jumps up and pounds the flames off the charred bread that is now unfit to eat. The next day at work, Marian says, "You know who started that fire, don't you?" I shrug my shoulders, turn from her, put on my headphones, and start my day. My mind is battling to understand these experiences with Marian. I have no doubt that there is something larger than me that should be a strong warning to stay away from her.

She asked for counseling from Papa Larson and after meeting with her, he comes to me and says, "Donna, I'm not casting one demon out of her. If I do, she will end up in worse shape than she is right now." He shares with me the Scripture in Matthew 12:43-45 about what happens when you cast out an unclean spirit. He continues, "She wants the dark powers she has so she can pour out revenge on her ex-husband."

I think I'm beginning to understand. She doesn't really want Papa Larson's help, my help, or Jesus' help. Papa Larson is firm: "She is a very dangerous woman and you need to stay away from her." I hear the truth in his words, but I care about her and our friendship at work. Papa Larson sees my hesitation to heed his warning and continues, "Donna! The devil wants you to put the pedal to the metal. He wants to keep you running in circles to care for those who don't want help. In the meantime, there's someone out there who is crying for help and you're too busy trying to care for the one who doesn't."

Wow. This hits me hard. I know he is right, and that I need to meditate on this and live it out, but it isn't easy when you really care for someone. Eventually, my time with Marian comes to an end, but for a totally different reason.

There's another person I am working with whom I grow to love dearly as a friend. She is in the Catholic church and our conversations are really interesting. Her name is Kathy, and she is quite the character. I love her personality, which is very outgoing and painfully honest sometimes. She is full of energy and enthusiasm for life. "You know," Kathy says to me, "I watch Christian TV and just laugh at some of the things they say and do." Since I don't watch Christian TV, I can't relate, but I just listen to her. She and I become fast friends, and I share with her about my experiences with Jesus and the Holy Spirit. She is very engaged and interested.

Poppa Larson asked me to write my testimony for the First Assembly of God Church quarterly info magazine. They "spotlight" a church member who shares their testimony for the congregation. Kathy graciously agrees to edit my written draft and I am grateful for her input and corrections to my grammar and spelling. Also, it is a way for me to share my personal story of Faith with her as well as the Gospel in a way that isn't like Christian TV. I appreciate our friendship and love her more and more every day.

One day, Marian comes to me and asks me to go on a trip with her to Rome, Italy. My goodness! "No, I am so sorry," I tell her, "I cannot do that." I'm thinking, *first of all, I do not like to travel and secondly, I have no desire to go to Rome…especially with you.* It's after lunch when I overhear Marian ask Kathy to go with her. Kathy jumps on it and soon, off to Rome they go.

My position as a transcriptionist and my desk are changed while they are away. I am now seated across the aisle from Marian and working as the receptionist when she comes back to the office. Several days after her return from Italy, our office manager informs the whole staff that Marian suffered a nervous breakdown and is in a mental facility for treatment.

My heart breaks for her. There is nothing I can do to help at this point because she doesn't want to give up the things that are killing her emotionally, spiritually, and physically. Since she wants these demons, they in turn inflict upon her constant thoughts of revenge against those who've wronged her and suicidal ideations. She has shared with me how she's been thrown around the room by this "unseen force" in her home causing multiple cuts and bruises. I'm devastated to see the state she's in yet I know I have to let go of the friendship.

The good news is, I am sitting at the desk right in front of Kathy. Oh my, this is not good because all we do is talk and laugh. Our friendship continues to grow, especially in the things of Jesus.

A Sudden Move of God?

I come home from work feeling troubled in my heart and mind, so I go straight to my room. I feel compelled to surrender to God, yet again. "God, if you want me to stay single, I'll stay single. If you want me married, I'll get married—and if you want me to move to Timbuktu, I'll go!"

I hear the Holy Spirit speak to my heart, "Donna, you will be married by the end of the year." I am in shock.

"God," I say, "I'm not dating anyone, how can this be?." I think, *It's May, and I'm not dating anyone, and December isn't that far away.* I wonder if that was God speaking or my own desire. As unpredictable as it sounds, I believe it came from God because I have really been working on building my two-way relationship with Him and praying for the ability to hear His voice. I decide to just put that idea on the shelf and take things one day at a time.

Several weeks go by, and I'm talking with Dan. We've spoken frequently throughout the year and a half we've been apart, and it is so nice to hear his voice. One of us brings up the idea of me visiting Ohio. We end our conversation and I immediately begin to pray. "God, if this is of you, open the door, but if it is not, close it TIGHT." Vacation time, reasonably priced bus tickets, and a place to stay are what I need to all come together as my sign for an open door. Within a few days, everything falls right into place! Vacation approved, check. Bus tickets, check. Staying with his mom and dad, check.

Being welcomed by Momma B and Papa Bob is a miracle. I hurt their son when I left for a visit to New York and didn't come back.

A year and a half later, on July 4th, I am in Cincinnati, Ohio, with Dan. My heart is racing. I'm not the same person I was when I left. I am now a radical Pentecostal sold-out-to-Jesus woman. I hug Dan and feel this warmth of love wrap around my heart for him, and it seems to envelop my whole body. I feel love coming from him also, yet it is guarded. I understand it; I left him and he was devastated. I have no idea where this relationship/friendship is going, but it's wonderful being with him.

Vacation time up, it's time to go back to New York. Dan arranges for me to fly so I don't have to travel by bus. It is so difficult leaving him again. I don't want this man who is very special in my life to slip through my fingers and out of my heart again. As I travel back to New York, I feel such loss and grief. My mind is in a whirl of confusion. *Are we supposed to be together? Is this the end or the beginning of something?* I guess I'll find out—I just have to put my trust in God my Father.

Dan and I begin conversing regularly. One night, we begin talking about getting married. It's crazy, we agree, as we don't really know each other. I'm different now and think that he doesn't know the new me—I am not sure he can live with me. We talk about our marriage ideas but make no set plans.

> "God, if this is of you, open the door, if it isn't, close the door TIGHT."

This is certainly something I must pray about AGAIN. "God, if this is of you, open the door, if it isn't, close the door TIGHT." While praying, I hear the Holy

Spirit whisper, "August 27th Do not speak it, Dan will confirm it." I obey, and don't say anything to anyone.

The following evening, we're talking and Dan says, "How does August 27th sound for a wedding date?" Dropping the phone, jumping up and down in excitement, and holding my hand over my mouth so I won't scream, I pick the phone back up and tell him I got the same date in prayer. I also say, "Yes!"

My dear Dan loving me being me (even when I'm goofy)

Oh my, August is only weeks away. I also find out that he'll be turning 30, which I didn't realize. I feel like I'm in a dream. Surrendering everything to Jesus is amazing. He arranges everything and I'm just along for the ride. A month and a half after my 4th of July visit, I'm in a whirlwind. So many arrangements to make in a very short time! I quit my job, dispose of furniture, buy a simple wedding dress and pack up all my belongings into my silver Buick Apollo.

My mom, brother, my dearest friend Kathy and I are now headed to Ohio for a wedding. Momma B. arranges everything. On August 27th, Dan's 30th birthday, we are standing in the Wesleyan Church in Milford, Ohio, exchanging our vows, and the next thing I know I'm married to this wonderful man. I am overjoyed with love for him and just know he loves me too, sincerely, like my dad loved me. I can't wait to begin life together in Ohio.

Knowing my ex and his wife, I was sure they wouldn't let my children come with me to Ohio for the wedding. Because it came together so quickly, I wrestled with whether to tell them before or wait until after. I decide to wait until after. Trying to figure out how to tell them I am moving to Ohio with my new husband is another one of the most difficult, heart-wrenching things I've ever done. I believe my marriage to Dan is God's will, yet the fear of telling them and the pain of losing them pulls at my heart in a way that no one can imagine. I'm overwhelmed with emotions—the joy of being married to Dan, along with the grief of leaving my children, family, and friends in New York. I feel joyful, sorrowful, fearful, excited, and like laughing as well as crying. How does one handle all of this? I feel like I'm going out of my mind. Help, God! I can't afford a psychiatrist! I start to think, *God, is this really Your will?*

Right from the onset of our marriage, I have doubts creeping in. *What have I done? Is this the right thing? God, did you really say August 27th? Did I make this happen somehow?*

After the wedding, Dan, my mother, brother, Kathy and I pile into my Buick Apollo and travel back to New York for a reception with family and friends. Then Dan and I visit my children, and I tell them, with their dad and stepmom present.

Gathering my kids around me, I say, "This is Dan. We were married a week ago and I am moving to Ohio."

Tricia, 12 years old, lets out a scream, "No!" as she runs and throws her arms around me and bursts into tears. My heart breaks into a million pieces for her, her siblings, and for me. This is so much harder than I anticipated. *How can I bear leaving them in New York? As happy as I am to be with Dan, my heart feels like it's being ripped out of my chest. I hope they will visit us in Ohio. At some point, maybe even come and live with us.* Silent wishes in my heart that hopefully will become a reality.

Several days after meeting with my children, I'm off to Ohio to do my best at making our marriage a happy and blessed one.

It's only been a month since our wedding, and I want a divorce. Dan works all hours of the day and night. Because I hurt him when I left a year and a half ago, his heart is very guarded. His words and tone are harsh.

One day he says, "God put us together. This is a business arrangement. I expect you to get a full-time job so we can get two new cars." He also shares that he never wanted children because he never thought he'd be a good father. He never said he didn't want my children.

I honestly don't know how to take this statement and am too fearful to ask him to clarify what he means. I feel as though many of the things I went through with my mother I'm reliving in my relationship with him.

Get a job, transactional relationship, no empathy or understanding, separation from my children. How can this be?

Emotions swirl around me, and I feel like I'm going crazy. I'm physically sick with allergies, severe migraine headaches, and extreme fatigue. The thought of getting a full-time job right now makes me shudder. It seems as soon as I moved here, a hail storm of issues hit me at the front door.

I am standing in our bedroom, looking up to God in heaven as I cry out, "God, I can't take this, I want to go back to New York. I have no family here, no friends, and I desperately miss my children!"

As I crumple into a heap on the floor, He responds back to me in a whisper, "Donna, if you're committed to Me, I want you to commit to this marriage."

"This is not what I want to hear, God. I want to go back to New York," I cry out to him in earnest. I'm broken, devastated, my dreams of a beautiful marriage are crushed. Dan is distant, angry, and I can't do anything right in his eyes. He's not the empathetic, compassionate man I thought he was. He walks in the door from work and criticizes everything I do. The light is on in the bathroom, there's a dirty glass in the sink. No matter what I do, it isn't good enough. I'm sure it's to guard his heart, but mine is crushed and I'm pulling away from him in fear.

It's expensive to call New York, but I need to talk to my family, my children. When the phone bill arrives, I am terrified of his anger.

At thirty-five cents a minute, it doesn't take long for the charges to start adding up. I know I'm not perfect, and have a lot to learn about being in a Christian marriage. It's been seven years since my divorce and then I wasn't committed to Christ. *How am I going to cope? How do I commit to this marriage and obey God?* In obedience, I stay—but my heart is not in it, not one single bit. I want out, but seemingly, there's no escape. Where do I go from here? I don't know. *Help, God! I can't afford a psychiatrist, is my constant prayer.*

Help, God!

10

Release

It's infuriating. Church-goers and pastors are eager to "help" but many of their approaches don't work. I'm met with churchy clichés like: "You don't have enough faith;" "Let's cast out the spirit of rejection and loneliness;" or, "In all things be grateful." I'm shut down with, "Don't speak the negative." It is perplexing to me. How can a person get help if they can't talk about their pain and hurt? All the praying, fasting, and professing of my faith that I am happy, healed and grateful haven't brought the peace I need in my mind or my body. Changing churches doesn't help…the message seems to be the same. Maybe there is some defect in me that keeps me stuck in dysfunctional patterns of hurt, anger, and depression.

Things I am told at church: Repeated sinus infections are because I don't have enough faith; my allergies are determined to be demons of abandonment and rejection; my brokenness means I have demons that need to be cast out.

I'm desperate and agree to anything—no results, just the pain of feeling demon-possessed, damaged, and imperfect.

I find myself sitting on the floor in my living room screaming out, "Help, God! I can't take this pain. I can't bear being separated from my children. I miss my family. Was I really supposed to marry

> God, I need you more than ever but I'm not finding You! What do I do? Where are you in the midst of my desperation?

Dan?" All these things crashing through my mind overwhelm me. I become convinced that I don't know how to pray, nor do I want to. *Where can I go but to You for help? God, I need you more than ever but I'm not finding You! What do I do? Where are you in the midst of my desperation?*

Being new in the Cincinnati area, the only friend I've made here so far is Ruthie. I try to call her in my desperation but her phone rings with no answer. Crawling on the beige carpet and spinning as though I am going out of my mind, I finally stop and sit with my back up against the dark blue recliner. Folding my arms, I look up and say, "Ok, God, I guess it's You and me, AGAIN." Help, God, I need Your help. I can't do this alone.

It's another unbearable day. Alone and tired, I sit at the piano and begin to worship or should I say, try to worship. In the midst of my song, I hear His still, small voice say to me, *"Donna, why are you striving to be perfect? There's only One who's perfect, and that's Jesus, and you ain't Him. Give yourself a break. You're going to miss it. You won't be perfect until you get to heaven or Jesus comes back first. When you sin, confess your sin, come to me and I will forgive you. You are my daughter and*

I love you. Run to me and I will take care of you. I will comfort you and fill you with the joy you first experienced in your sanctuary in New York." I continue to worship, feeling grateful that my Father heard my cry for help and He came to comfort me in my distress. I know there's a lot of inner healing needed, but for now, I'm content right where I am, worshipping Jesus.

It's Sunday and I think perhaps I'll feel better if I try something different today and go to a church service that will be held in an old, refurbished barn. It's blisteringly cold and snowing hard. I was told not to wear high heels which might damage the beautiful wooden floors. Bundled in my warmest coat, wearing jeans instead of a beautiful dress, an old sweatshirt and my warmest boots, I walk in and wish it felt warmer inside, yet it does feel inviting.

Once inside, I am greeted by a dear sweet woman with the most precious smile. Her name is Pam and she escorts me to a table where volunteers are serving coffee and hot chocolate. The service is held up in the loft of the barn. The floors are shiny oak and so are the walls. Chairs are placed in rows facing the back wall. In the corner, I see a man with a guitar (I find out later is Pastor Steve Sjogren) sitting on a stool. He's wearing jeans, a sweatshirt, and sneakers with no socks, *interesting, I've never seen that before.* There's a mic stand and a music stand placed in front of him. He begins to sing worship songs to Jesus. There are about 50 people gathered together and we begin to sing, in unison, the most beautiful, melodic songs I've ever heard.

My heart is captivated by the sweet music. The words and melodies are easy to follow; no overhead lyrics, hymnbooks, or song sheets to follow along. Slow, deep meaningful songs flow from him as he plays and sings. The sound system permeates through every corner of the barn. I hang on every word of these songs I've never heard before: "Isn't He Beautiful" and "You Are Here and I Behold Your Beauty." They touch me deeply. I close my eyes and as I sing, the depth of the words he sings, touch my heart and fill my mind. Jesus, Prince of Peace, Son of God, Yes You are. You are here, and I behold Your beauty, Your glory fills this place. I feel wrapped in His presence like a butterfly in a cocoon. For the first time in a very long time, I feel I am home, home with my Jesus and home with kindred spirits who love Him.

Welling tears make me open my eyes. I begin to weep in the middle of worship. Just then, a man I've never met walks over and stands next to me. Softly, he tells me his name is John. He puts his hand on my shoulder. No words of condemnation, no judgments of any kind—he doesn't speak a word to me. He weeps with me as I surrender to gut-wrenching sobs and tears. I feel sweet love pouring out of him for me in a very safe, brotherly love kind of way. I'm broken into a million pieces emotionally. All I can think of is *thank you for letting me be real.* I'm sitting here on this cold, hard chair wearing jeans and bulky boots; snot and makeup intermingle and run down my face—and no one seems to mind.

"Take off the mask, let's be real, come as you are, you'll be loved" are messages I'm not familiar with. They are like salve to my wounds. I know in my heart this is where God wants me to be and that Vineyard Christian Fellowship will now be my home church. Pastor Steve has a small group in his home during the week and I attend regularly. The same sweet music and presence of the Holy Spirit permeates his living room and I can't wait to get here week after week. Twenty to thirty gather together, eager to worship and learn more about Jesus Christ and the gifts of the Holy Spirit.

In an effort to get some counseling and prayer, I meet with Pastor Steve and a lay counselor, Ron, to talk about my depression issues and difficult marriage. Pastor Steve looks at me and says, "Donna, you're very angry."

"I am not," I say, thinking, *No way, I do not want to be an angry, hateful woman like my mother. It's not true.*

"Yes, you are, and you really need to deal with it." He and Ron are both adamant that I have an anger problem. They tell me that depression is often caused by suppressed anger turned inward. I don't believe them and leave feeling extremely frustrated. *Dan is the reason for all the hurt in our marriage. He is a workaholic, never home, I'm alone all the time!*

Now what? Where do I go from here?

Pastor Steve and Ron must have been praying for me because now, the next day after our meeting, I can feel the anger and rage building up in me. There's no denying it. I call the Vineyard church office to set up an appointment. "I am really angry and I need to deal with it TODAY," I say to the receptionist on the phone. Within the hour, I arrive at a building where the Vineyard church has its corporate offices. I'm shown to one of the small offices.

I walk in and notice the wooden-framed couch with soft cushions on it and a matching chair with an ottoman. Two wooden end tables with a lamp on each one are placed on each side of the couch. The chair and ottoman are placed in the middle of the room. Ron says, "Hi, Donna." I'm feeling a bit nervous, but anxious to start the process. It's just Ron and me, but I'm feeling safe as he directs me to sit in the chair in the middle of the room. After a minute of small talk, Ron says, "Have you ever seen a Bataka bat?"

I have never heard of this before, but it doesn't look too strange, this bat he retrieves and hands to me. It has a big black plastic handle connected to a very wide, long piece of foam formed in the shape of a large, wide sword. It is covered in red fabric. He explains that this "Bataka" bat is used to help release anger and aggression. It's sturdy, but soft enough that it won't cause any damage upon impact. I'm seated in the chair with the ottoman placed in front of me at knee height, and Ron encourages me to begin swinging the bat down to hit the ottoman. He wants me to think about things I'm angry about, say them out loud, and pummel the ottoman. He stands behind me with his pen and notebook.

I start to lightly tap the bat onto the ottoman, saying, "I hate my mother. I hate that she got with Stan, a married man, right after my dad died. I hate Stan." Ron tells me to let the anger all the way out.

Whack! The intensity of my taps increases.

WHACK! I slam that bat full force onto the cushion of the ottoman. WHACK, I hate my mother, WHACK, I hate that man who sexually molested me. WHACK, WHACK, WHACK!!! Ron stops every so often to offer me water and to pause for a little bit. I must be wearing him out. I'm energized. Give me that darn bat! I want to get rid of this stuff before I kill somebody.

The more I say, the more there is to say. The more I scream, the more excruciating memories rush to my brain and travel like electricity down my arms to explode into pounding the Bataka bat.

Nine hours later, I'm dripping in sweat and red in the face from the release of this rage, anger, and hatred. Specific incidents of trauma and abuse have flown out of me and into the abyss, things I had forgotten and tucked away in the recesses of my heart, secrets never spoken. I drop the bat and sit back in my chair, totally undone.

Ron begins to read back to me everything that had come out of my mouth. It's painful to hear and incredible how much toxic rage I had spewed. "You need to forgive your mother," Ron tells me. "Forgive her for having an affair and for everything. And you need to forgive those who sexually abused you." This is really HARD. I feel a fog setting in as I thank Ron and leave to go home. I am exhausted mentally, emotionally, and physically. I sleep hard.

Morning comes, I wake up and realize that I must call Ron. He agrees that I can come back and I head over to the office to begin another session with the bat, though my neck and shoulders are sore from yesterday. Maybe today won't take long.

More venom pours out of me. I hear myself and think, *Jesus, forgive me for harboring hatred, anger and being so unforgiving.* I know I must forgive those who hurt me, but there is more pulverizing the ottoman to do, more anger to express violently and decisively. I slam my bat for the next eight hours. I stop, and Ron seems to know it's time for me to begin the forgiveness part of my healing.

I pray, "God, I forgive my mother for the evil things she did to me, specifically the physical and emotional abuse. I forgive her for the time she bashed me with her fist in the back of the head for no reason. I forgive her for embarrassing me in front of Aunt Lee and her friends. Because You chose to forgive me of the evil things I have done, I choose to forgive the evil things my mother has done to me. Release her and help her come to know You so she can go to heaven and be with You and my dad."

Then Ron leads me in a prayer like this: "We command the effect of the curses spoken over Donna to become null and void in Jesus Christ's Mighty name." The "curses" are the terrible words spoken to me, which have struck me like curses on my life—like my mother telling me I was *stupid* and that I could not do *anything* right.

After both of these sessions I think, *Yay, I'm clean and free of all that rage and anger.* Little did I know this was just the beginning of peeling back the layers of hurt built up through the years.

11

"Your Word is a Lamp to My Feet"

It's Christmas Day around 7:00 p.m. and I'm standing in front of the phone, mustering up the courage to call my kids in New York. My God, I miss them terribly! As I look at the phone, fear begins to overwhelm me. What I expect to hear from their stepmom is making me sick to my stomach, and I'm trembling like an earthquake is shaking the ground underneath and everything around me. She is so critical, so vicious with me. Treating me much like my mother does, I feel every hot/trigger button within me being pushed all at the same time. Fortunately, the love I have for my kids overrides the intensity within and I make the call.

First one to answer is my precious son, Donald. In the course of our conversation, he begins to whisper into the phone. He tells me he is in the bathroom with the door shut. I picture him crouched on the floor, phone in hand, as he tells me his secret so dear to his heart. "Mom, do you know what our pastor said tonight? He said, 'Don't forget about Jesus at Christmas.'"

Overjoyed, I reply, "Donald, thank you for sharing this with me. Jesus truly is the reason we celebrate this season. Remember that Jesus loves you very much, and so do I. Never forget how much I love you, okay?"

Tricia and Tami are next in line and I cherish my visit with them. As soon as we're done, their stepmom gets on the phone. Here we go—every demeaning thing she can think of comes spewing out of her mouth at me. "Why don't you write more often? You're not responsible enough to care of your children, so they're not allowed to come for a visit. You can't do anything right where they're concerned. You're not responsible enough. Donald has special dietary needs because his kidney issues are so severe, we know you won't take care of him properly." Donald was diagnosed with kidney disease, was on dialysis and ultimately had a transplant.

I think, *How can I have Tricia and Tami come here to live or for a visit, and Donald not be allowed to come? That would not be fair to him. I want to be with my kids.* These thoughts are running through my mind in the midst of listening to her go on and on about how "imperfect" I am. All the hot buttons are being pushed again all at the same time.

Through her constant barrage of insults and complaints, I try my best to keep from exploding in a rage at her. This "one-way" conversation finally ends. I hang up the phone and the momentary joy I felt after talking with my kids is completely gone, and I'm trembling on the inside. The eruption of anger, boiling up from deep within, presses in on me.

What's happening? I just went through hours pounding out my anger and rage with that stupid Bataka bat. I drop to my knees and pray, "God, enough of their stepmom and dad! If they would just get hit by a truck, I could have my kids back."

That still, small voice permeates my thoughts, *"No Donna, that's not my way. You need to forgive them and go on."* Wiping away tears, I'm torn. I want them dead; I want my kids. How can I forgive her and their dad? Knowing what to do but not wanting to do it wages war within my mind. My thoughts are scattered. Hate, forgive, love…God this is hard. Guilt ridden, I hate myself in the process.

Finally, I take a deep breath and ask for help to do what He asks me to do. "Okay, God, I choose to forgive them for the evil they are perpetrating against me and my children. You forgave me so much more…how can I hold unforgiveness and resentment in my heart? I forgive them for berating me, keeping my kids from being able to visit me, and for all the heartache and pain they have caused since my children went to live with them."

God, I know my kids are hurt by my absence and I so desperately want them to know that I love them with all my heart. I know all of my shortcomings as their mom and I hate what I put them through. My God, what these poor kids have endured at my expense. Heal their pain, their hurts Father. Touch my kids and draw them to You first then to me.

I hear the Holy Spirit whisper, "Donna, you need to forgive yourself." *How do I do this? Help me Father.*

I begin, "Father, I forgive myself for being an imperfect mother to my children. I forgive myself for the rage, hatred and thoughts of wanting their dad to get run over by a truck."

Then I speak to myself out loud, saying, "Donna, you are forgiven for rage, hatred, bitterness and malice against Dave and his wife. 1 John 1:9 says that if You confess your sins, He is faithful and just to forgive and cleanse you from ALL unrighteousness. That settles it, I am forgiven, cleansed and free from the guilt and shame associated with it."

With a huge sigh, I can feel the pain dissipate and leave as I give it over to God. Here I thought that all the anger and rage had been released. That bat and I had worked so hard! Honestly, I thought for sure I wouldn't have to deal with any of it again. Well, I guess this is a process I'll have to walk through, darn it!

> With a huge sigh, I can feel the pain dissipate and leave as I give it over to God.

———◇———

It's the middle of the week, Dan's already at work, and I'm standing alone with my coffee cup in hand, gazing out the bay window into our back yard. So much beauty in the midst of a subdivision. Lush oak trees, cottonwood trees, honeysuckle, weeping willows, and more greenery surround the back of our home, giving such privacy and peace. The bird feeder is alive with activity; sparrows, finches, chickadees, mourning doves, bluejays, and too many other species to count. I watch with fascination the interaction between them as they flitter around each other to get their share of the seed. Squirrels, raccoons, and stray cats are frequent visitors also. And I have a "pet" female turkey I named Gladys, who comes close and practically eats out of my hand. I love these creatures and do my best to protect every one of them.

In a sense, they've become like my children. As I gaze upon each creature, each tree, I think about what a creative, unique God He is. Hundreds of birds fly around with their individual colors, markings and voices. The different types of trees with no two leaves created the same. How much more has our Father taken the time to create and shape each one of us with our unique personalities, hair color, eye color, height, weight, etc. No two of us alike, even if twins or quintuplets, all unique in some way. I stand in awe and wonder at His beauty.

Enjoying my time reflecting on my Father's goodness, without warning, I hear the Holy Spirit whisper, "Donna, get a piece of paper and pencil and make two columns. One column, title, 'The Lies My Mother Told Me'. The second column, title, 'The Truth According to the Word of God'." Grabbing the first piece of paper I can find, I set up the columns.

The Lies My Mother Told Me	The Truth of the Word of God
You're stupid	2 Timothy 1:7 — *For God did not give us a spirit of timidity, but a spirit of power, of love and of self-discipline.*
You can't do anything right	Philippians 4:13 — *I can do everything through him who gives me strength.*
You'll never amount to anything	2 Peter 2:9-10 — *But you are a chosen people, a royal priesthood, a holy nation, a people belonging to God...*

I would never have come up with this assignment on my own, but I am already feeling enlightened by it.

Then He speaks to me, saying, "I want you to rewrite the old scripts written on your mind. When you start to hear and have the thought that you're stupid, do not believe it nor wish it away.

Rather, gather your strength and confront it, saying, 'No, that is a lie. I am NOT stupid' Then speak out 2 Timothy 1:7. Replace 'you're stupid' with this: 'For God has not given ME, DONNA, the spirit of timidity or fear, but of power and of love and of self-discipline. I have a SOUND MIND.' Command the words 'you're stupid' to leave, in Jesus Christ's name."

Beginning now, you can make these affirmations for yourself: I am NOT stupid. I have the mind of Christ. I can think, I can learn and I can discern between right and wrong. I can discern between the negative voice in my head and the truth of God's word. "Your Word is a lamp to my feet and a light to my path" (Psalm 119:105).

Our Father God is so amazing. He broke into the middle of my morning to give me an awareness and method to counteract the negative thoughts running through my mind. If someone insinuates that you can't do anything right, wave your hand over your head and say, "NO, I can do ALL things through Christ who gives me strength."

> "Your Word is a lamp to my feet and a light to my path" (Psalm 119:105).

Discerning Truth from Error

In the Bible, discernment is a way to perceive God's will and what is good and acceptable. For example, Romans 12:2 tells us, "Do not be conformed to this world, but be transformed by the renewal of your mind, that by testing you may discern what is the will of God."

Colossians 1:9-14 is a powerful Scripture to pray for yourself, family, and friends on a regular basis for help to grow in discernment and wisdom. I change the wording to make it a personal prayer. Here's an example:

Colossians 1:9-14: "Father, fill me/us with the knowledge of Your will in all spiritual wisdom and understanding. Help me/us to live a life worthy of You that I/we may please You in every way. Help me/us to bear fruit in every good work, growing in the knowledge of God, being strengthened with all power according to Your glorious might so that I/we may have great endurance and patience, joyfully giving thanks to You who has qualified me/us to share in the inheritance of the saints in the Kingdom of light. Thank you for rescuing me/us from the dominion of darkness and bringing me/us into the kingdom of the Son You love, in whom I/we have redemption and the forgiveness of sins."

One thing I know for sure, the closer we draw near to God in worship, prayer and reading the Word, the clearer and more concise discernment becomes.

I'm in awe of His mercy and goodness. I'm not perfect, I don't always obey, but He loves me anyway. He will NEVER leave me. He's always by my side. That's one thing I know about My Heavenly Father. He is with me everywhere I go, and He cares about my well-being, even when it's neglected by myself or others. This is what is in store for you when you give your heart to Jesus.

Help, God!

12

Help, God! How Do I Start?

With or without Jesus, there will always be difficult, confusing, and sometimes tragic situations at some point in your life. One day we're okay, the next...the death of a parent, loss of a child, a devastating diagnosis or injury. Facing struggles without Him to rely on is nearly impossible. That's why, without Jesus, we are often compelled to look for help from alcohol, drugs, sex, emotional eating, a "Daddy hero," retail therapy, and empty promises of other people...even church-going imposters. Never, ever do I want to struggle alone again without Jesus, never.

With wonder, I think, *could it have been an angel that walked into the grocery store when I was being molested?* He certainly heard my screams for help in the pit of hell when I died of an overdose. All my life I searched for a hero, someone to rescue me like the prince in *Sleeping Beauty* or *Snow White*. I was convinced I had to find someone like my daddy who loved me unconditionally–until one day he was gone. Little did I realize that my Heavenly Father was my unseen rescuer, my eternally reliable hero. From tragedy to triumph, hatred to love, He was, with me all through my life. Here's the kicker: I couldn't see it clearly until after writing Part I of this book.

Even though I turned from my faith in Him and religion to find my own way, I never denied God. Yes, I landed in a pig pen, much like the prodigal son in the Bible who left home, squandered his father's fortune, and was reduced to working on a pig farm, Now I see that even in my darkest times, He never turned His back on me. He waited patiently for me to come to the end of my rope, in total weakness and despair, where I fell into His arms of love, leaving my dirty past behind.

The before-Christ and the after-Christ lives are interwoven, part of the whole tapestry of our being. There will be days when depression, shame, and guilt hit hard and locks us up in a silent prison. Jesus Christ, through the power of the Holy Spirit, continues to help break through, unraveling the twine that's twisted together within. Surrender is not a one-time act—it literally must continue over and over as each day presents the need. He continually reveals an area where we need to forgive, or where we're holding onto an offense someone spoke against us. When we surrender again, the silent, dark prison walls break open and the light comes bursting through again bringing joy and peace.

> He wants us to remember that He reveals to heal, not to condemn. Conviction from the Holy Spirit brings freedom. Condemnation from our enemy, Satan, brings oppression.

He continually draws us into the light of freedom. He wants us to remember that He reveals to heal, not to condemn. Conviction from the Holy Spirit brings freedom. Condemnation from our enemy, Satan, brings oppression.

The Holy Spirit, the Perfect Counselor

The original Greek definition of the word *counselor* means: "One who is called aside to help, to encourage and assist." We can depend on the Holy Spirit as our counselor to guide, instruct and encourage us every day in the ways of Jesus.

I've seen counselors, cried on a friend's shoulder, and sought wisdom from others inside and outside the church. Many times I cried out, "Help, God! I can't afford a psychiatrist!" Today, my dependence is on Him, not on a parent, a pastor, a therapist or my spouse. If their counsel is sound and lines up with Scripture, I will take it to heart. I watch, wait, and listen—then decide on my course of action before moving forward.

In 1 Timothy 4:16, we find, "Watch your life and doctrine closely. Persevere in them, because if you do, you will save both yourself and your hearers."

There are many false prophets and "New Age" counselors who have infiltrated the church and many a young believer has been snared by false teachings. Things like, "…you have diverticulitis because you're full of bitterness."

"…so that your faith would not rest on the wisdom of men, but on the power of God" (1 Corinthians 2:5).

One dear woman I know was told, "Now you received prayer for

153

healing, so go home, throw away your meds and believe that you're totally healed." This sweet woman, standing in faith, believing she was healed, had cancer and died not long after. My heart breaks when I see so many of my brothers and sisters in Christ hurt by such cruelty. Proverbs 14:15 warns us: "The simple believe anything, but the prudent give thought to their steps."

God's Word is where to go for counsel. Here are some of my favorite Scriptures about this. As you can see, Jesus said we would receive another Counselor, the Spirit of truth.

John 14:15-17: "If you love me, you will obey what I command, And I will ask the Father, and he will give you another Counselor to be with you forever, the Spirit of truth."

John 14:23-25: "If anyone loves me, he will obey my teaching. My Father will love him, and we will come to him and make our home with him. He who does not love me will not obey my teaching. These words you hear are not my own; they belong to the Father who sent me. All this I have spoken while still with you. But the Counselor, the Holy Spirit, whom the Father will send in my name, will teach you ALL things and will remind you of everything I have said to you. Peace, I leave with you, my peace I give you. I do not give to you as the world gives. Do not let your hearts be troubled and do not be afraid."

> "Do not let your hearts be troubled and do not be afraid."

1 John 4:18 reads, "There is no fear in love, but perfect love casts out fear. For fear has to do with punishment, and whoever fears has not been perfected in love." Separation from God is the ultimate punishment or fear.

All You Need is Love

Jesus says, "You shall love the Lord your God with all your heart, and with all your soul, and with all your mind". Jesus also says that this is the first and greatest commandment (Matthew 22:37). Jesus also emphasized that one should love one's neighbor as oneself.

Unfortunately, many churches and preachers teach just the opposite, putting love of neighbor as yourself before loving God. This is not God's truth, and therefore never works out the way you'd want it to.

It's impossible to love others as yourself until you fall in love with God through His Son, Jesus Christ. It is imperative to love Him FIRST. Without loving Him, we can't obey Him, we can't forgive others or forgive ourselves. It's His love within us that gives the power and the desire, through the Holy Spirit, to obey.

God knows your situation. He knows exactly what you need. I'm thankful for my earthly dad. Because he was so gentle and compassionate, I think it made it easier for me to love God and accept His unconditional love.

Every one of us have past experiences and relationships that impact how and when we surrender to Jesus' love. Maybe your dad was the abuser and your mom was the compassionate one. Maybe your dad was absent from the family. This can make it harder to see God as compassionate, loving and near instead of distant. Many of us see God as a harsh judge, sitting on His throne just waiting for us to mess up somehow so He can whack us with that Bataka bat....

Here's a tip for you: Forgive the imperfect parental influences in your life. I've witnessed many of my friends struggle with Father

155

God because they think he's like their earthly father, often seen as too strict, judgmental and unforgiving. I had to recognize that my dad was a human being, kind to me yet flawed and imperfect. Looking back, there were times when I felt betrayed by him because he sided with my mother, who was clearly in the wrong. He was in the Navy during WWII and he cussed like a sailor. He wanted all of his kids raised in the Catholic church, apparently without stopping to think about all of their teachings. What an eye-opener to realize my dad wasn't perfect and I needed to forgive him along with my mother. What I do know is my dad loved me and he loved God and he loved His Son. I have full confidence that I will be reunited with him again one day.

Our Heavenly Father is PERFECT! He wants a relationship with you, right now, right where you are. You might think you've committed THE unpardonable sin. That's a lie of the enemy to prevent you from surrendering to Christ and to keep you in a state of panic and anxiety. Don't believe the lies. Invest time seeking the truth in God's Word, take the Scriptures that apply to you and speak them over your life.

Forgiving Can Be Hard, but It's Always Freeing

In all honesty, there are times when I'm so angry I don't want to forgive. I want to hold on, going over and over it like a broken record running through my mind. Thoughts like, *She hurt me, I can't believe she said that about me. Why didn't I tell her off instead of walking away, beaten down? I don't ever want to talk to her again.* When that happens, my favorite go-to Scripture

He pours into me the willingness to forgive and shows me how to do it.

is Ephesians 4:31-32: "Get rid of all bitterness, rage and anger, brawling and slander, along with every form of malice. Be kind and compassionate to one another, forgiving each other, just as in Christ, God forgave you." As I pray and ask God to help me get rid of all bitterness, rage and anger, He is eager to answer. He pours into me the willingness to forgive and shows me how to do it.

If you believe in Jesus Christ, say this: "Satan, you're a liar, you're the father of lies. My father is the Father of TRUTH. Jesus said if I confess my sins, He will forgive me and cleanse me. I'm CLEAN. NOW GET LOST SATAN IN THE NAME OF JESUS CHRIST. I REFUSE TO ACCEPT YOUR LIES ANY LONGER."

Jesus died to save you from the flames of hell. He wants to pull you out of the pit of despair into the presence of His peaceful, loving home. He's waiting with open arms to welcome you in.

My Child, Where are You?

He takes delight in His children, even you, no matter how long or far away you wandered. When you walk away, He stands at the door, looking, waiting, anticipating your return. When you finally surrender your life to Jesus, excitement and joy fill the heavens.

Picture this: The Father is standing at the door. He keeps looking, waiting. Suddenly one day he sees a figure walking up the very long path towards home. He's not sure who it is at first—as the figure approaches, but is still a good distance away, he recognizes who it is…Oh, Oh, IT'S MY SON! IT'S MY DAUGHTER!

EXCITEDLY he runs into the house, asks the cook to prepare a big meal. He tells another to check his room to be sure it's dusted and ready. Then He RUNS—He runs with all his might to greet his son, his daughter with arms wide open. With a booming, joyful voice he shouts, **"You're home, you're home, my child. I've been waiting for you. I've missed you and I've been waiting, waiting patiently for your return."**

Welcoming you with hugs and kisses on each cheek, he walks beside you, so pleased you are where you have a deep sense of belonging.

There are garments. One by one, He gently covers you with His robe of righteousness. He fastens the belt of truth about your waist, places the helmet of salvation upon your head, puts the shoes of the gospel of peace on your feet, and fills you with the Holy Spirit. He places in your hand a sword, which is the Word of God and places a ring on your finger. This is the authority given in Jesus Christ's name to be wielded against the enemy. You are NOW covered from head to toe with the Armor of God (Ephesians 6:10-18).

You, child of God, please know that He's standing at the door, looking and waiting especially for you. He loves you so much that He gave His one and only Son for you, so that you will have everlasting life.

RUN. Run my friend, with all your might, and as though your entire life forever depends on it—because it does.

"Let us approach the throne of grace with confidence, so that we may receive mercy and find grace to help us in our time of need" (Hebrews 4:16).

"Therefore, having been justified by faith, we have peace with God through our Lord Jesus Christ" (Romans 5:1).

EPILOGUE

No matter what, there is nothing you've done that will separate you from God's perfect love. This profound truth is what I've come to clearly see from my journey of reflection in writing this book.

By the grace of God, my prayer was answered and I feel His presence in my life, and His encouragement for me to reach out and help others. As I've shared with you, there are scars and triumphs to carry, each a testament to the person I've become.

Life today is sweet. My siblings and I are very close and love each other deeply. I'm so thankful that all of us know Jesus Christ as our Savior and Lord and will be together for eternity.

In 2014, my precious sister Debby had a heart attack and passed away. She was truly a soldier of the cross, the brave one in the family who never gave up on any of us becoming born again. We miss her beautiful smile, her artistic, "hippie" flare, and look forward to seeing her again.

Near the end of her life,
Mom wanted a pajama party with all her children around

In 2017, my mother passed away of esophageal cancer. She came
to know Christ before she transitioned. It was meaningful to both
of us to heal our relationship (it's never too late!). Not wanting
to burden her children, she settled all of her financial affairs,
gave away her belongings, paid for her funeral, and wrote her
own obituary. None of us could doubt her deep love for us. She
left this earth totally forgiven and extended forgiveness towards
others. Our prayers for her were answered at the very last minute.

My oldest daughter Tricia and I have a beautiful relationship. It's been over 30 years since I've seen my other two children, Donald and Tami. My prayer is that they come to know Jesus Christ. Nothing would make me happier than to reconnect with them.

Dan and I are retirement age but stay busy, to say the least. We've navigated countless storms in our 42 years together, and the Lord always sees us through. I'm grateful for all God has given us— our home, family, friends and our precious kitties. We both look forward to what He has in store for us in the future.

I'm so thankful for all that Jesus has taught me and is still teaching me. I know you, dear readers, are not seeking "more information" but are hungry for healing, connection with God, and practical wisdom—lessons from a spiritual being having a human experience. I promise to honor God's calling, which is empowering me to work on my next book, also with the "Help, God!" theme. I hope you'll join me again!

May God Bless,

Donna Benedict

Help, God!

ACKNOWLEDGEMENTS

My first and foremost gratitude goes to Jesus Christ. Over 20 years ago I was impressed upon to write my story through the Holy Spirit. In May of 2024, during my prayer time, I heard the Holy Spirit whisper, "It's time, get it done, time is running out and your time is running out. Write that book." Within the week, I was on a roll as He put together everything needed to get the project done, especially the perseverance to do it.

Thank you to my husband Dan, my daughter Tricia, and all my family and friends for your encouragement, strength, and sensitivity which helped get me through some of the toughest days emotionally. You listened day after day as I talked about stories you've heard a million times. Thanks for believing in me that I could do it. I love you all with my whole heart.

Barbara Dee, of Suncoast Digital Press, Inc., I could never have done this without you. As soon as I heard from the Lord to write this book, I "just happened" to hear about you, along with a strong endorsement. You believed me that the Holy Spirit put it on my heart to write this memoir and you agreed it would be helpful to others to hear it. I'm thankful for your direction, teaching (loved your Master Class!), editing, and encouragement to keep going. The times I felt that I was the worst writer in the world, you shared with me that even Stephen King needs an editor. You worked tirelessly, even through two hurricanes, to get us to our goal. Thank you so much, Barbara Dee and the Suncoast publishing team for all you've done to get this story out to those who are hurting and broken. I'm looking forward to the next book and know it will be easier because of all you've taught me, a first-time author.

Elaine Ruskin, my dear friend and a former English teacher, thank you for believing in my vision to write this story. You were the first person to invest your time and energy in viewing me as a writer, which I could not see in myself. I'm so blessed to call you not only a friend, but a sister in Christ.

Special thanks to Val Mott for your photography, which gave me what I needed for my book cover and in my speaking career. Your friendship and support mean more to me than you could imagine.

New Heights Church staff, New Life Vineyard, and those who took time to pray for me, thank you. When I needed the "army of prayer warriors" to help me through this journey, all I had to do was pick up the phone. What an incredible group of people you are and I am so grateful to each one of you and blessed to be a part of this church family.

To my readers, thank you for taking time out of your busy lives to read my story. I am confident that you will be able to apply some of the lessons I share about how you can heal and grow in your relationship with Jesus Christ and with our Heavenly Father, our hero.

ABOUT THE AUTHOR

Donna Benedict is an ordained minister through Christian Global Outreach Ministries. She served as "Pastor over Prayer and Prayer Teams" at New Life Vineyard in Hamilton, Ohio. She has served as a lead worship vocalist on various worship teams for over 30 years throughout the Cincinnati area. Her true gift is leading others into true, intimate worship of Jesus.

Additionally, she developed workshops including "The Gifts of the Holy Spirit" which she led several times in women's conferences, Women's Aglow meetings and Bible studies.

Donna is clear on her priorities. Matthew 6:33 says, "Seek first the kingdom and His righteousness and all these things will be given to you as well." For Donna, this means seeking God first, even as she spends time every day with family and friends and her precious kitties—she has taken in many a rescue, nursing them back to health. Some of her hobbies are fluid art, jewelry making, reading, and writing.

Donna enjoys to speak to groups of any size and enjoys her "retirement" by traveling to conferences, churches, womens' groups and schools to share her message of positivity and hope. Her desire is share with others how to recognize the voice of the Holy Spirit, have courage to walk in the authority of Jesus Christ, and to build or reconnect with their Heavenly Father through Christ.

To contact Donna: HelpGod.db24@gmail.com